VANGUARD OF VICTORY
The 79th Armoured Division

Frontispiece: *Major-General Sir P.C.S. Hobart KBE, CB, DSO, MC, founder and Commander-in Chief, 79th Armoured Division.*

Vanguard of Victory

David Fletcher

The 79th Armoured Division

LONDON   HER MAJESTY'S STATIONERY OFFICE

Contents

© *Crown Copyright 1984*
   First published 1984

ISBN 0 11 290422 X

Printed in the UK for HMSO
Dd 736187   C30   4/84

Introduction

A yellow triangle apex down, outlined in black, displaying the head of an aggressive-looking bull with red nostrils and tips to his horns; the device, or Divisional Sign, of the 79th Armoured Division. This beast was in a sense the offspring of a full-bodied creature which served to identify the 11th Armoured Division. The connection between the two was Major-General Sir Percy Hobart, an outstanding, outspoken and therefore controversial officer, whose stormy career spanned both World Wars. Commencing as a Royal Engineer, Hobart transferred to the Tank Corps in 1923. The new corps, which was permanently established in September of that year and granted the Royal status a month later, embodied the spirit of progress in the post-war army and thus became a natural magnet for young officers of vision, among whom Hobart was in the van.

Rising fast, Hobart became Inspector of the Corps in 1933 and in the following year he took charge of the newly created 1st Tank Brigade, a position which enabled him to exercise his unique gift for command and to develop his theories on the employment of armoured formations. The outbreak of war in 1939 found him in Egypt, moulding and training a unit that was to be an inspiration to Britain in the oppressive years ahead, 7th Armoured Division, the Desert Rats. A clash of personality with the GOC in Cairo, H.M. Wilson, lost him the post and he returned home to premature retirement. He served for a while with the Gloucestershire Home Guard until, rescued from oblivion at the insistence of Winston Churchill, he was selected to raise and train the newly formed 11th Armoured Division in 1941. Yet again fate intervened; following a bout of illness and despite Churchill's objections he was judged unfit to command a fully-fledged division in action and the 11th lost their man. At this point his reputation for thoroughness in training paid off for, like the 7th

before it, the 11th Armoured had an enviable reputation, so when it was decided to raise two more armoured divisions in 1942 Hobart was appointed to train one of them. As it turned out, there were simply not enough tanks available in Britain for two more divisions and the War Office reduced the requirement to one, the 79th, which Hobart duly commanded.

By way of contrast to his previous appointments, which had been built up virtually from nothing, the 79th Armoured Division was formed by drawing off units from other formations. It was Hobart's task to weld them into a cohesive whole and give them a new sense of identity. As first formed, its armoured element was the 27th Armoured Brigade, which comprised three regiments, the 4/7 Dragoon Guards, 13/18 Hussars and the East Riding Yeomanry.

The majority of tanks were Covenanters, fast light cruisers with a reputation for overheating and general unreliability which rendered them fit only for training. In the normal course of events these would undoubtedly have been exchanged for Cromwells or Shermans before seeing action and the future of the division would have been no more or no less remarkable than any of its fellows. Instead, within seven months of being formed, the division was given a new role which made it at once a unique and fascinating part of the British Army.

By the spring of 1943, Allied operations in North Africa were approaching a successful conclusion. With the Axis armies defeated south of the Mediterranean it was obvious that any future offensive would have to be mounted on the European mainland, first through Italy and later, when adequate force was available, in northern France, the only place where the Western allies could confront and defeat those major elements of the German Army not committed on the Russian front. Despite considerable pressure from various quarters, this final invasion was delayed until the summer of 1944, when sufficient equipment would be available and sufficient numbers of troops concentrated and trained for what must be the greatest allied effort of the war. The crucial factor in the success of the entire scheme was the initial landing. Unless this could be carried out effectively the whole affair would be doomed and the war could drag on for years. Past experience gave little cause for optimism. Every ingredient in the recipe for success had to be included, and this is where the 79th Armoured Division fitted in. One of the primary lessons learned at Dieppe was that armour should not be slapped down on the beach at the outset, all that could be done first by way of sea and air bombardment and conventional infantry assault must be attempted to pave the way for the tanks, that is conventional tanks. What if a variety of special machines could be provided to answer the needs of the first wave, to give immediate fire support to the infantry and also perhaps undertake the gruelling work of the Engineers? In March 1943 Hobart was summoned to a meeting in London at which General Sir Alan Brooke, Chief of the Imperial General Staff, outlined his plan to raise a peculiar armoured division charged with developing, training and using a range of special-purpose armoured fighting vehicles that would lead the Allies into France. The formation chosen to undertake the work was the 79th Armoured Division. The right man for the job their commanding officer –Major-General P.C.S. Hobart.

By 1943 standards a typical armoured division was composed of one armoured brigade along with an armoured-car regiment and divisional artillery and an infantry brigade and ancillary arms. Experience had shown that this formed a manageable and practically self-sufficient whole. By virtue of its highly specialized role 79th Armoured Division was a different matter. As first reorganized it comprised one tank brigade, one armoured brigade and an assault brigade Royal Engineers along with a special experimental unit. During its two-year war-time career it expanded to include a number of other brigades all deployed in various special types of Armoured Fighting Vehicles (AFVs). Thus all its units worked in armour although they never operated as a collective entity, being split up and seconded to other formations as occasion demanded.

A detailed history of the division was published in 1945, written by a serving officer. Since then a number of other works have been dedicated to it, dealing with the historical and technical aspects of its activities. It would be impertinent to claim that this offering replaces any of them. Rather it is intended to be complementary in the sense that it offers the reader the very best of an amazing collection of photographs now held in the archives of the Tank Museum.

The Museum collection includes many of the special-purpose armoured vehicles associated with the 79th Armoured Division, the Sherman Crab, Sherman DD, Matilda CDL, Buffalo, Weasel and Churchill Crocodile.

1 On the beach

Of all types of military operation none is more fraught with difficulty, more hazardous, than the opposed landing from the open sea. Throughout history from Caesar's landing at Deal in 55BC to Abercromby's assault at Aboukir Bay in 1801, the odds against success have been high. With the fickle ocean at their backs the assaulting forces are in action as soon as they are in range from the shore and the tricky business of disembarkation and wading ashore has to be effected under fire, often against an enemy who is prepared for their coming and securely dug in. The two operations mentioned were successful but history can show as many examples of failure as success. As with most military actions the chances of success are in direct proportion to the amount of careful planning that has been carried out but the unpredictable moods of the sea inject an extra factor that must never be discounted. Even when they establish a beachhead the soldiers and sailors cannot take their ease, the follow-up must be continued with vigour until the initial forces are well in land and their support can be landed and organized to maintain the offensive.

For an island nation, or indeed a continent that is not directly threatened by the enemy such actions are often a prerequisite of victory; however until the present century it seems not to have been a subject considered worthy of serious study. This failure may have been the result of the traditional rivalry between the seaborne and the landbound arms, or a consequence of the view that each landing was a unique event that could not be looked at in the light of previous actions. Thus it seems that no cumulative body of experience was ever built up yet for all that the problems remained the same.

The advent of mechanization has by no means solved these problems. In both the First and Second World Wars amphibious operations have been very risky and this has made them at once dramatically memorable and a focal point for historical study. The first great seaborne assault of modern times was the Gallipoli landing of 1915. Legend has tended to obscure the fact that the initial phase of getting ashore and forming a beachhead was by and large successful. That this probably owed much more to the courage and tenacity of the fighting troops and sailors than the conduct of the high command is not entirely relevant except to the extent that they chose to put their men ashore on the tip of the peninsula at first, instead of the narrow neck further along, which would have avoided the need to secure a vast tract of inhospitable land that could otherwise have been cut off. The operation failed because the army did not capitalize on the success of their own initiative, but waited around for orders from a Commander-in-Chief who stayed aboard his command ship, out of touch with the situation ashore.

1 *Gallipoli as it never was; a war artist's impression of the River Clyde at V Beach. This prototype landing ship was the only innovation in an otherwise conventional amphibious assault. In reality few who left the ship in daylight made it to the shore. The ship's boat in the foreground shows how the majority landed.*

Apart from the increased scale of firepower afloat and ashore, Gallipoli was in essence much the same sort of operation as Aboukir Bay over one hundred years before. The troops were mostly sent ashore in open boats; they scrambled over the gunwales and waded to the beach to meet the enemy almost muzzle to muzzle (in much the same way in fact, apart from the boats, as their comrades in arms were doing on the Western Front at the same time). Yet within two years things would change dramatically and for ever.

Although no comparable action took place in the European arena before the war ended (the Zeebrugge assault being a raid rather than a true landing), new techniques were developed that showed how things would be in the future. This was the result of a projected landing on the Belgian coast, known to those who were involved, under a cloak of secrecy, as the Hush Operation. One of the primary tactics of warfare is the outflanking movement, by which one catches an opponent unawares from the side while he is facing stoutly to his front. In eastern France, where one end

of the line lay against a neutral border and the other rested on the Channel coast, this could be done in one of two ways. Swiss sensibilities could be ignored, with all that implies, or a force could be put ashore behind the German lines from the sea. This latter course was favoured. The idea was to land a force big enough to be a nuisance and support it with an attack along the coast that would join up with the Hush attackers and open up a corridor to an expanding beachhead which would envelop Antwerp and provide a new northern front for the allied armies. Under pressure from both north and west the enemy would be pushed back and defeated. Since the landing depended for its launching, let alone its success, on the result of the Third Battle of Ypres it was never mounted, for when that offensive bogged down at Passchendaele Hush was called off and a lot of very frustrated men went back to the trenches. That there was such disappointment is due in no small part to the highly specialized nature of the proposed operation and to the degree and intensity of training that had been carried out to prepare for it. What makes Hush so interesting is that it was proposed to employ tanks as part of the assault force. This decision alone must have given the scheme an unreal air to those in high command, it was the dream of enthusiasts . . . of visionaries . . . madmen.

2 *A glimpse into the future; one of the great pontoons at the bows of two monitors during trials in the Thames Estuary.*

3 *A Mark IV male tank fitted with the special ramp for tackling the sea-wall during the Hush Operation.*

When Hush was planned the tank, as an instrument of war, was hardly a year old and it had not come very far in that time. The Mark IV of 1917 was only a slight improvement upon the original Mark I. Its combat record was unimpressive and its reliability suspect, yet here it was, a prime mover in an action of considerable daring that, should it succeed, would solve a tactical impasse of nightmare proportions. For all its promise the tank gave the proponents of Hush a few headaches as well. For one thing it had to be transported to the beach and landed, then it had to climb a sea-wall all under fire – this was no easy exercise. For the landing the Royal Navy devised and built three enormous pontoons, each 550 feet (167.34 metres) long and tapered at the rear to wedge between the bows of a pair of heavy gun monitors which, lashed together, provided the propulsion, steering and fire support for this unwieldy assembly. Three tanks would ride at the bow of each pontoon and once they had bumped ashore at the head of the troops they faced the sea-wall.

Two features of this sea wall meant trouble for the tanks: the surface would be thick with slippery seaweed and the top, curved outwards like the crest of a wave, presented an insurmountable obstacle. To deal with the first problem the tanks were given special toothed spuds that fitted to the tracks and dug through the slime to bite into the concrete. The lip required more sophisticated equipment. It took the form of a small portable wedge-shaped ramp on wheels which the leading tank shoved before it up the sloping wall until it jammed under the overhang. The tank then

disengaged and climbed over the ramp onto the esplanade to fight its way inland.

Some of the tanks were also fitted with external winches that were used from the top of the wall to haul up wagons and guns. As an object lesson in planning and development Hush was second to none. In the long term, details of the modified tanks are unimportant; what mattered was the appreciation that special circumstances required special solutions.

The period between the wars was one of almost total stagnation in the development of amphibious assault techniques. The actual tanks improved beyond recognition, as did the theories of tactical employment, especially in Britain, where the pattern was set for the rest of the world. The idea that tanks had a part to play in landing from the sea was virtually ignored; indeed, with the memory of Gallipoli still fresh, the whole idea of large-scale amphibious operations was regarded with the utmost suspicion in regular army circles. The only organization to give the matter any positive thought was the Royal Marines. They steadily developed and tested a series of prototype self-propelled landing craft capable of carrying tanks and they even went so far as to investigate methods of handling them across various types of beach surface.

When the German forces evicted the British Army from mainland Europe in 1940 it was apparent that it would be only a matter of time before the return trip was made. From that time the development of tank landing craft went on apace until all that was lacking was the practical experience of landing in action. No matter how realistic they might be,

4 *The prototype landing craft MLC10 dropping its stern ramp off Portsea Island with two light tanks Mark II aboard.*

5 *A Churchill III on the beach at Dieppe. It appears to be burning but the initial cause of its demise was no doubt the broken track.*

training exercises could only teach so much. In August 1942 a large-scale raid was mounted against the enemy-held port of Dieppe. Although a number of directly offensive motives were included in the planning, like the cutting out of enemy vessels and a scheme to draw a large portion of the Luftwaffe into the fight and destroy it, the primary purpose was to test the effectiveness of the German defences and carry out a combined armour and infantry landing under fire, for the lessons it could offer. This largely Canadian operation was the action debut of the new Mark IV infantry tank, the Churchill. These tanks, serving with the Calgary Regiment, were slow 39-ton machines with heavy armour protection but relatively weak guns when compared with contemporary German and Russian tanks. The beach at Dieppe is steep and shingly, the worst possible surface for heavy tracked vehicles, but preliminary tests on similar beaches in Britain had revealed that they were quite capable of getting across if certain measures were taken to assist them. First of all the exhaust pipes were modified and raised well above water level to prevent the engine from drowning in the shallows, while the leading tanks were fitted with a carpet laying device which unrolled beneath the tracks to provide a firm path. To get off the beach the tanks had to climb a vertical sea-wall and to assist them here teams of Royal Canadian Engineers were trained to destroy sections of it with explosive charges. Three tanks were also adapted to carry flamethrowing apparatus with which they could neutralize pillboxes and other defensive structures

6 *Bert was one of the tanks that made it onto the promenade. It too has lost a track and is shown being examined by its captors.*

that might survive the initial bombardment. In the event things did not go according to plan. Many landing craft were unable to maintain the timetable and some batteries that covered the beaches were not put out of action by the initial Commando raids so that the tanks were landed higgledy-piggledy with the leading infantry on to a beach that was swept by an intense volume of fire. Many of those that got

ashore were stranded on the shingle or had their tracks shot away by anti-tank gunfire, including the flamethrowers, while the engineers were all but wiped out before they could do their work.

Those tanks that did make it over the sea-wall were unable to get beyond the esplanade due to further concrete obstacles in the streets and although virtually immune from penetration by German anti-tank guns, except on their tracks, could only surrender when their ammunition ran out. From the tanks that were landed only one crewman was able to return home when the recall was ordered and the Germans were left in possession of some twenty-eight of the latest British tanks in exchange for relatively light casualties.

The memory of Dieppe is a dark but glorious one in Canadian and indeed all Allied recollections but despite the cost the lessons had been learned and this time they were not forgotten. The immediate reaction was to consider as unwise the landing of tanks with the leading infantry before the immediate defences had been subdued. For the same reason the desirability of large landing craft lingering on the beach after unloading was frowned upon while in the Canadian ranks the heavy loss of life among the engineers caused minds to turn to methods of using tanks for this dangerous but essential work.

From Dieppe onwards technique and experience grew rapidly. Operation 'Torch', the landing on the North African coast, was largely carried out under United States control. It suffered many of the vicissitudes of inexperience and over-confidence but it was relatively unopposed. During 1943 a succession of landings on Sicily and the Italian mainland, although increasingly well defended since the Germans were learning, too, gradually settled the finer points of technique which were to prove invaluable during the last great invasion of Fortress Europe in 1944.

7 A Grant tank fitted with Scorpion flail equipment climbs onto a rocky Sicillian shore during the landings.

8 A British manned Sherman on the beach at Salerno.

2 Specialized armour

We have already seen how, before the tanks were a year old, it had been found necessary to modify some of them to overcome the special problems posed by the Hush Operation. By the time the war ended many more specialized roles had been found for them as their potential was appreciated. This should have led to an obvious conclusion but for one reason or another it was almost ignored. The landmine has generally been considered an effective counter to the tank; one of the first modifications to remedy this was carried out on a mark IV tank in 1917. A pair of stout beams stuck out ahead of the tracks with a large roller suspended from the leading end of each, it was hoped, would detonate mines in its path and spare the tracks. A few old tanks were stripped and strengthened in 1918 to serve as a portable causeway upon which fighting tanks would cross the Canal du Nord while other tanks were provided with fascines, large bundles of sticks bound tightly with chains, that were released from the top of the tank to fall into wide trenches, serving as stepping stones to prevent the tanks from falling in. Tanks were adapted to carry or tow stores and transport infantrymen in relative safety and devices were produced to cut wire or carry mortars. Some types saw action, others were never used, but the fact that they were tried at all gives some indication of the potential of special purpose tanks.

By the time the war ended special supply or troop-carrying tanks were undergoing trials while a multi-purpose Royal Engineers tank was in the prototype stage. This was a modified Mark V** heavy tank fitted with a hydraulically operated jib which could be used to lay a bridge, place an explosive charge or trail a mine-sweeping roller as required, while, of course, the jib itself had a more direct application as a field recovery crane. Yet another problem was solved on Armistice Day when one of the new troop-carrying tanks, a Mark IX fitted with large air-filled drums, floated about on Hendon reservoir. Thus many of the devices later used with great success by the 79th Armoured Division had already proved necessary in an earlier conflict. The pity of it is that this development virtually ended with the war and before long the very need for them was forgotten.

The new generation of tanks that entered service after the war had no special fittings. Some experimental types designed in 1919 with built-in amphibious capability appeared but they were never developed and the twenty years that separated the two World Wars saw tank design progress rapidly without comparable progress in armoured support equipment. A few bridge-layers appeared and duly vanished while the Royal Engineers settled for unarmoured lorries and when infantry was transported they used similar truck-bodied half-tracks. The only field which seems to have attracted the inventors was that of light amphibians, tanks fitted with permanent floatation chambers and marine propellors. However, apart from their value as reconnaissance vehicles they were hardly suitable for crossing anything but inland waterways and only then against minimal opposition. Some attempts were made to make ordinary light tanks float by the addition of detachable bouyancy devices and a Light Tank Mark II was tested at sea with a pair of pontoons strapped to the sides and an outboard motor on the back. It took part in at least one landing exercise but despite later developments involving tanks up to cruiser size it was always a time-consuming business fitting the floats and caused even more trouble when they were dropped before action on the farther shore. Otherwise inter-war development was spasmodic and uncoordinated. Odd examples appeared of searchlight tanks, mine ploughs

9 *Mark II light tank T880 complete with Straussler pontoons and a Johnson outboard for amphibious trials. Notice how the exhaust pipe is raised to stay clear of the water.*

10 *The old way: teams of Sappers with mine-detection equipment clear a gap during a training exercise.*

11 *The new way: a Matilda Scorpion Mark I moves up in the desert. The tall poles on the rear deck are for station keeping, to enable following tanks to trail their leader through the dust cloud raised by the flail.*

and trench-crossing contrivances made from cable drums but, since there was no specific body charged with development, ideas burst forth or fizzled out according to the whim of individuals or units.

This situation remained true for the early part of the Second World War except that now more thought was given to the special-purpose machines that might be required. If they proved useful, they were produced in larger numbers and included in the establishment of the unit that operated them. The wide expanse of the Western Desert was well suited to tank warfare. British armour dominated a much larger Italian force before March 1941, when Rommel arrived with the Afrika Korps. One of the best methods of denying ground in this relatively featureless landscape was the laying of extensive minefields and the only practical response was the use of manpower for mine detection. Even with the aid of detection equipment, the task of clearing mines was time-consuming and dangerous. Mechanical aids were therefore developed and although these could not do the job as thoroughly as the manual method they proved adequate for armoured warfare when a percentage loss could be accepted in the interests of speed. Tanks appeared with a variety of fittings including rollers mounted on frames and flails. These latter took the form of a power-driven drum mounted across the front of the tank from which were suspended lengths of chain or weighted wire tendrils that thrashed the ground ahead of the tank as the drum rotated. The fame of these rollers was such that Major A.S.J. Du Toit, the South African engineer who evolved them, was transferred to Britain to develop his ideas further.

Other schemes originated in Britain. At Christchurch modified tanks with bridge-laying apparatus appeared and others were adapted to push larger bridges into position. Both were revivals of First World War ideas and another was reborn when the old Canal du Nord scheme reappeared. They had originally been known as 'sacrificial tanks' since they were abandoned once they had formed the causeway, but they were now called ARKs since their flat tops reminded some of the famous aircraft carrier *Ark Royal*. Based on a turretless Churchill they were fitted with hinged ramps and used to fill anti-tank ditches or prop themselves against sea-walls so that other tanks might climb across. Another revival was the search-light tank; it mounted a special turret containing a powerful arc lamp with rapid moving mechanical shutters which blinded onlookers by causing rapid expansion and contraction of the pupils. Used in pairs they could effectively isolate a pillbox, permitting the attackers to move in close through the dark sector between the lights. Developed in great secrecy under the ambiguous code name of Canal Defence Lights (CDL), they were hardly known outside the chosen regiment that trained on them.

Operation Jubilee, the Dieppe raid, saw the introduction of the tank-mounted flamethrower and the carpet-layer into British Service and both were retained and improved but the most important result of that operation was the appreciation of the need for an engineers tank. This recognition, which followed on from the ideas of a Canadian officer, Lieutenant J.J. Denovan, led to a variety of tanks being examined for their suitability. The Churchill was finally chosen on account of the thickness of its armour, the spaciousness of its hull and, especially, because it had side access hatches in the track frames. The great advantage of this feature was that it enabled demolition engineers to dismount in relative safety and place their charges under cover. This aspect was later over-shadowed by another development based on the principle of the spigot mortar devised by Colonel Blacker. It was developed from the simple but effective Blacker Bombard produced for the Home Guard and in its later form became a short-barrelled mortar for fitting in place of the main armament of a tank. This fired a powerful demolition charge nicknamed 'Flying Dustbin', which proved immensely effective against concrete emplacements. The weapon was fitted to production Churchills of the Mark III or IV type which henceforward became known as Armoured Vehicles Royal Engineers (AVREs). This basic type was then further adapted to permit it to carry a host of other engineer plant capable of being operated from within the tank. These included improved carpet-laying devices called Bobbin, various types of demolition placing attachments, fascines, mine-clearing equipment and even bridges. Considering that it was an improvisation, the AVRE more than justified itself in action making it probably one of the most important items ever to fight on the Normandy beaches.

Despite the apparent lesson of Dieppe it was soon realized that there was nothing intrinsically wrong with the idea of having tanks arrive on the beach alongside the first infantry wave. The difficulty was in getting them there. A 200-ton landing-craft could carry nine medium tanks right up to the beach but it presented an enormous target. Each craft that was disabled on its final approach meant nine fewer tanks available to the attackers. At close range even a light gun could wreak havoc and the risks were simply too high. One solution might have been to have divided the tanks among large numbers of smaller craft but there would never have been enough of them and in any case they would all have had to be launched and loaded off the beach instead of making the channel crossing under their own power and this would have created terrific problems. The best answer would be to have the tanks swim ashore by themselves but the difficulty here was just as daunting. A special amphibious tank was by definition a light-weight that might be knocked out by the least potent of anti-tank weapons, but a normal fighting tank of the 1943 period could hardly be expected to float; or could it? The problem was finally

12 *Straussler's masterpiece, the collapsible floatation screen fitted for initial trials to a Tetrach light tank as it chugs out, under outboard power, into Langstone Harbour.*

13 *Fitting Straussler floats to a Crusader Mark I. The turret attachment is an Atherton Jack, which supports the pontoon while soldiers struggle to fit it in place.*

solved by an émigré Hungarian engineer, Nicholas Straussler. Given adequate displacement anything would float and Straussler exploited this by surrounding the tank with a collapsible canvas curtain of sufficient size to support it in the water. Initial experiments with a modified Tetrach light tank proved the idea to be sound and in due course the Valentine infantry tank was chosen as the production vehicle.

It was a 16-ton tank of reasonably modern design with proven reliability despite being under-gunned by contemporary standards. Its great virtues were an easily waterproofed hull and the fact that it was available in large numbers since it was rapidly being replaced in front-line service by the Churchill and Sherman tanks that would bear the brunt of the fighting for the rest of the war. In its modified form the Valentine was moved in the water by a singe propeller driven off the main engine. This system was called Duplex Drive and the modified tanks were known as DD tanks. In normal sea conditions they were perfectly safe and reasonably manoeuvrable, they could be launched straight down the ramp of a landing craft and swim directly to the beach where the canvas screen was collapsed and the gun swung into action. Unlike the pontoon system already tried on Crusaders, the floatation screen took up no more room than a conventional tank, it added very little to the overall weight and once folded down it made little or no difference at all to the normal function of the tank as a fighting machine.

This then was the situation when 79th Armoured Division was ordered to take on its new role. All over the country individual regiments were training with their particular charges, progressing steadily to the desired state of readiness but lacking the essential collective direction that could ensure cooperative success. It was now up to Hobart to oversee development and standardize training methods to bring his incredible menagerie to the same fine pitch of perfection and united self-esteem that he had brought to all his former creations. His own sense of achievement would be further enhanced in the knowledge that this time his duty would not end when the training was over; this time he would continue to serve them in action.

3 Training to perfection

In its new guise as the parent formation of specialized armour in the British Army, 79th Armoured Division was composed almost entirely of armoured regiments, always excepting of course the divisional support units, Royal Army Service Corps, Royal Army Medical Corps, Royal Electrical and Mechanical Engineers, Royal Signals and so on. Initially these armoured units comprised the original 27th Armoured Brigade already mentioned, 30th Armoured Brigade and the 1st Assault Brigade, Royal Engineers. In addition the 43rd Royal Tank Regiment was detailed for experimental work. For various reasons these units were widely scattered. Some were already in being and training at suitably secluded locations while the new creations required equally secret sites suited to their particular roles.

A good example of the former case was 35th Tank Brigade, which operated the Canal Defence Light tanks. They had been training in Britain since 1941 using Matilda infantry tanks fitted with modified turrets to house the lighting apparatus. It was planned to convert to the Churchill in due course but the choice finally settled on an American tank, the Medium M3 Grant, the main armament of which was contained in the hull structure. It therefore had a positive advantage over its rivals because it retained an adequate offensive capability to supplement the light. Lowther Castle in the Cumberland Fells south of Penrith was their home, a place so isolated and forbidding that it kept its secret even from the British Army, not to mention the enemy. Rumours of science-fiction-style death rays began to circulate when vivid flickering beams were seen playing round the hills at night. New arrivals reporting to brigade headquarters looked around in vain for familiar tanks but they had to sign

14 *Night-time in the Lowther Hills and a Grant CDL aims its flickering beam at a farm building.*

the Official Secrets Act before they were admitted to the compound where the tanks lay heavily shrouded during the daylight hours. The initiation rites involved sessions with bright spotlights in darkened rooms but once the principles had been absorbed and night descended the covers came off, the tanks moved out onto the rolling fells and the lights were switched on.

Moving in sections, the tanks advanced against a selected target while every thirty minutes a crew member, wearing special asbestos gloves, was obliged to replace the consumed carbons in the lamp. Despite the fact that the flickering action failed to have the desired effect on all eyes, the value of the basic principle was established with but one serious limitation. It was soon realized that an enemy gunner on the flank could see every move in stark silhouette and this rendered the system as much a liability as an advantage, except in certain specialized circumstances, which in the event never occurred.

Like the CDL, the DD or Duplex Drive device was already in being when the division was formed. However, it was March 1943 before full-scale production was under way of the Valentine version and these were issued to 27th Armoured Brigade from April onwards. The site chosen for initial training was Fritton Decoy, a large lake on Lord Somerleyton's estate near Lowestoft in Norfolk. In order to practice launching from the bows of LCTs, the REME constructed special concrete jettys with hinged ramps made from Bailey Bridge components. In the calm of this reed-garlanded duck-pond the crews practised their art. Of course some sank and it was necessary to train the men to escape in an emergency. To this end some large concrete tanks were built and filled with water in which men were trained to use submarine escape apparatus. It seems,

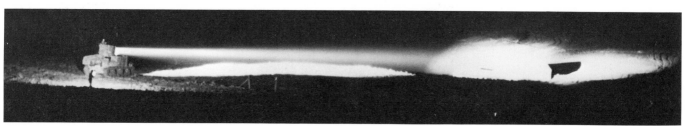

15 *The fan-shaped glare from the CDL arc lamp is demonstrated here as the Grant in the foreground throws its light at four companions on a distant hill.*

16 *A DD crewman demonstrates the modified Davis Submarine Escape Apparatus which could save a life in a sinking tank.*

17 *An LCT (4) with a full load of DD Valentines heaves to in Loch Fyne ready for launching.*

20 *With all the crew, except the driver, gathered on deck, this DD Valentine prepares to follow its comrades ashore.*

18 *DD Valentines on the deck of an LCT start their engines in preparation for launching.*

19 *A DD tank eases itself carefully into the water from an LCT (3).*

21 *A view from the bow of an LCT showing the extension ramps which helped to keep the propellor from damage.*

however, that, apart from the luckless driver, the crew preferred to make the voyage 'on deck' so to speak, accepting the risk of being shot in preference to being trapped in a sinking tank and drowned.

Once the basic handling problems had been mastered, it was essential to practise with the tanks at sea. The original site chosen was Loch Fyne in the Sound of Bute, probably because there was already an amphibious training establishment based on Inveraray. Here the tanks were launched from the ramps of the landing craft to form up and make for the shore. In due course the training was concentrated on

the south coast and a special wing was established at Stokes Bay in the Solent where, despite the risk of being spotted by enemy reconnaissance flights, mass launchings and landings were practised and practised again until a high degree of efficiency had been achieved. Further along the coast, off the Dorset village of Studland outside Poole Harbour, was one of the experimental defensive installations which released petrol onto the surface of the sea to form a flame barrage against enemy landing craft. In the event that the Germans had devised similar devices, a DD tank was modified to permit it to pass through unscathed. Blessed

22 *Three tanks are ashore, the others still afloat. Even in the calm waters of Loch Fyne the limited freeboard of the Valentine DD is evident.*

23 *Valentines coming ashore during an exercise at Stokes Bay. The screens have been dropped and the turrets traversed forwards to bring the gun into action.*

24 *Valentines with their screens down sitting on the shore at Stokes Bay. Notice the raised exhaust pipe, lifebelt stowed on the turrets and the crewmen in their lifejackets.*

with the uncompromising name of Belch, it consisted of a small pump which drew water from the sea and released it as a spray from the rim of the screen. Belching away the tank steamed sedately through thick clouds of murky smoke and flame with nothing worse to show for the experience than an oily stain around the waterline. To test more conventional defences an unmanned DD was used as a target for 75mm and machine-gun fire, which tore holes in the canvas and bent a few stays but failed to sink it.

25 *Belch in action: a suitably equipped DD tank comes safely through the blazing water in Studland Bay.*

Notwithstanding the many attributes that made it an ideal tank for conversion to the DD role, the Valentine was not up to the standard of contemporary allied tanks in terms of gun power and armour. Hobart therefore insisted that the equipment he sent ashore on D-Day should be adapted from current service tanks in so far as this was possible. In DD terms this could only mean the American Sherman, although a typical example weighed about 30 tons against 16 or so for the Valentine. With the height of the canvas screen raised the Sherman proved just as seaworthy, indeed more so in a heavy sea since the added weight below the surface tended to stabilize it better. Power in the water was increased by fitting two propellers driven through a gear train from a toothed ring on the idler. These propellers could be folded upwards out of harms way when the tank was ashore. Another advantage with the Sherman was that the gun could be trained forwards without interfering with the screen; the Valentine was obliged to swim with the gun pointing backwards. The technique for landing in action was to collapse the forward end of the screen as soon as the tank grounded in the shallows, enabling it to fire forwards while the raised rear end sheltered the engine deck from following breakers. The three original regiments of the 27th Armoured Brigade were soon joined in training by others, the 15/19th Hussars and the Nottinghamshire Yeomanry of the British Army, the 1st Hussars and Fort Garry Horse of Canada and the 70th, 741st and 743rd Tank Battalions of the United States Army. These latter units trained alongside the British and Commonwealth troops and represented the only elements of the entire British menagerie of specialized armour to be adopted by the United States forces for D-Day.

The low-lying coastal plain around Orford on the Suffolk coast is a sparsely populated region at the best of times but

26 *A Churchill ARK Mark I serves as a ramp on a section of sea-wall for a gun tank to climb. A scene during training at Orford.*

27 *The primary weapon of the Armoured Vehicle Royal Engineers was the Petard. The loading technique is demonstrated on this Churchill Mark III AVRE.*

28 *Once it is loaded the Petard reverts to a horizontal mode, ready for firing.*

29 *Nubian, an old Churchill Mark II, demonstrates its ability to pass through a demolished obstacle.*

in the early summer of 1943 it was quieter than usual. In a spirit of patriotic self sacrifice the scattered population accepted enforced exile in order to provide the army with a vital secret training ground. In their place came the 79th Armoured Division or at least that large part of it which included all the other specialized units of the assault force not so far mentioned. Here were constructed full-size concrete replicas of the many features of Hitler's Atlantic Wall that it was their business to overcome, along with samples of all the curious steel obstacles that Rommel was

busy planting along the beaches of northern France. Daring low-level passes by RAF aircraft on the enemy held coast brought back detailed photographs of ugly wrecking devices; tetrahedra, Czech Hedgehog and Element C, as they were christened in Britain. Unless these were overcome everyone might as well stay at home. Besides being virtually the Home Headquarters of the Division, Orford Training Area became the base for the 30th Armoured Brigade consisting of the 22nd Dragoons, the 1st Lothian and Border Yeomanry and Westminster Dragoons with their Crabs and the three regiments of the 1st Assault Brigade Royal Engineers, that is the 5th, 6th and 42nd Assault Regiments R.E. with their AVREs.

24

The Armoured Vehicle Royal Engineers was of course the Churchill. The majority were of the Mark IV type with a cast turret, the remainder being Mark IIIs with the angular welded type. During training some of these tanks retained their regular armament, the six-pounder gun and two Besa machine guns, others were seen with the main armament removed pending the arrival of the new weapon, the Petard. This stubby twelve-inch calibre piece replaced the six-pounder in the turret but it could only be loaded externally, by breaking the barrel like an air rifle. Sliding hatches replaced the normal hinged type above the hull machine-gunner's position, through which the round was loaded. Each tank could carry twenty-six rounds of Flying Dustbin, a dumb-bell shaped object weighing forty pounds, which could deliver a twenty-six pound charge up to a range of 210.31 metres (230 yards), although in practice the effective range was not much more than 73.15 metres (80 yards). The effect when they did strike home was devastating. One well-placed shot could bring a house down, a series of them would shatter the stoutest concrete wall or bunker. The Petard was equally useful for destroying steel beach obstacles. Alternatively these could be reduced by perforating them with 75mm armour piercing shot from a conventional tank which then proceeded to squash the weakened structure flat. The other great virtue of the AVRE was its adaptability to a variety of specific subsidiary roles. Each tank was provided with a set of multi-purpose brackets on the hull from which could be hung a selection of fittings to enable it to perform specific tasks. The variety was

30 *A Crab attempts to uproot a beach obstacle by shoving it over.*

31 *A Churchill AVRE carrying a Small Box Girder Bridge. The extra weight tended to push down the nose of the tank and it was an unwieldy combination to operate.*

baffling, as invention improved upon invention a whole series of attachments were perfected for laying bridges, carrying demolition devices or mine-lifting ploughs and launching the fascines. Most impressive of all was the version equipped with a Small Box Girder Bridge (SBG).

Mention has already been made of the true bridge-laying tanks; they were highly specialized vehicles which transported and launched a bridge automatically in the face of hostile fire if need be, by mechanical or hydraulic means. They were complicated, costly and therefore relatively rare, definitely not to be squandered. Their peculiar advantage was that they could not only lay a bridge, they could lift it up afterwards and use it again if required. Such units were issued to conventional tank brigades and were not the direct responsibility of the 79th Armoured Division. However it was foreseen that there could be situations in an assault when a bridge might be needed as a semi-permanent fixture, one that only needed to be dropped once under fire and not recovered until much later if at all. Hobart's team therefore devised a method of carrying a 30-foot (9.14 metres) Small Box Girder Bridge on the front of a tank for short distances. It was slung at an angle of about 60 degrees braced by wire

32 *A Small Box Girder Bridge being emplaced by an AVRE during training.*

from a small winch on the rear engine deck. The tank approached the obstacle, be it a ditch or steep wall, and the bridge was released to fall, if all was well, in the right place while the tank continued as a conventional AVRE.

The fascine was a complementary device. The 1943 pattern was little different from the 1917 style used at Cambrai although it often had a core of hollow tubes. It rested on an angled cradle on the front of the tank, secured by cables with a quick-release device above the turret. It was an awkward thing to transport, since the combination of fascine and cradle obscured the view of the entire crew and the commander was obliged to scramble onto the top of the bundle and direct the driver from there, except of course in action when they had to manage as best they could. There were three important uses for the fascine: it could fill a trench or anti-tank ditch, rolling off the cradle which was discarded afterwards; it could be used as a step to enable an ARK, for instance, to position itself effectively against a high wall; and it also served as a cushion to break a fall. In this last case it may be imagined that a bridge has been laid against a high wall. The fascine tank climbs up and drops its burden at the foot on the far side which reduces the drop and receives the tank with enough deflection to prevent the crew from being severely jolted.

33 *Carrying the fascine on the rear deck of a tank was not a good idea. It rested on the exhaust pipes and was liable to catch fire.*

34 *The fascine in use: a Churchill IV with deep wading kit fitted demonstrates the technique for trench crossing.*

All other considerations aside, the primary purpose of the AVRE was demolition. It has already been explained that the Churchill tank with its doors in the sides was an ideal vehicle for carrying demolition teams under fire. They would dismount to place their charges under cover and then return to the tank, which backed clear and detonated the charges at a safe distance. Even this could prove costly in trained men under some circumstances and a number of schemes were tried to permit the tank to place the charges mechanically. They were arranged on a light framework attached to the front of the tank which drove up to the obstacle and pressed the device against it. The whole assembly was then released while the tank backed off to fire it. Rejoicing in such peculiar code names as Goat, Carrot and Onion a whole catalogue of contrivances was developed but few if any were used in action. AVREs were also used to provide a number of other services which will be touched upon later.

The principle of the ARK has already been described. The UK Pattern appeared in two basic types, the Mark I, with short extension ramps to bridge an (8.3 metres) 28-foot gap, and the Mark II, with longer ramps which could span (14.33 metres) 47 feet. If occasion demanded it could also carry a fascine.

One thing obstacles such as ditch, wall, blockhouse or tetrahedra had in common was that one could see them. Formidable they might be but there was no denying that they were visible. The mine on the other hand is a sly enemy. Unless it is part of a well-defined field it is a very difficult thing to detect and extremely tricky to neutralize without considerable risk. Mines come in all shapes and sizes from small anti-personnel to large anti-tank types. All were lethal enough in their own right but the anti-tank mine was a serious impediment to mobility, which was the key to victory. Among the many devices invented to counter it, the tank-mounted flail seemed to be the most promising. Early examples have already been mentioned but the majority of these had the severe disadvantage of requiring a separate engine to drive the flail rotor, which in turn meant that the flail tank was deprived of its turret in favour of the extra motor housing. So although the principle was firmly established, by 1943 it was clear that there was room for improvement. The Baron and Marquis, the Scorpion and Lobster had all been tried with varying degrees of success but the best answer was the Crab. This consisted of a normal Sherman gun tank with the flail rotor projecting on a pair of arms from the front. The flail was driven through a series of shafts and universal joints from the tank's main engine so auxiliary structures were kept to a minimum. Once a minefield was suspected the Crabs arrived and began the slow business of flailing across. Moving at a Crab's pace of 2½ kph (1½ mph) the first tank beat its way along, clearing a lane 2.74 metres (9 feet) wide as the flail chains struck and detonated the mines in its path. They did

35 *The Matilda Baron was an earlier type of flail fitted to a turretless tank. The flail rotor was also designed to be used as a rotary digger to demolish earthworks.*

not get every one; mines sunk in hollows or sheltered by folds in the ground remained to take their toll of following vehicles but the ratio of detonations was high enough to be acceptable in action. Tanks were unable to fire whilst flailing so they worked in teams, each tank clearing a lane while its brothers sat on the sidelines engaging likely targets with their 75mm guns. The usefulness of the Crab was increased by fitting wire cutters to the ends of the rotor drum; these tore up entanglements that would otherwise ensnare infantry. The biggest drawback with the flail was that it could not be used to search for minefields. Besides being far too slow as a vanguard in the general advance, constant flailing of unsown ground would quickly wear out the chains and reduce its effectiveness when mines were found. To this end other varieties of anti-mine attachment were devised for both Sherman and Churchill, mostly in the form of rollers. These were developments of the oldest method of mechanical mine clearance. Some were designed by a rival organization in Surrey, the Obstacle Assault Centre (OAC). The most effective was made by the Canadians and was known optimistically as the Canadian Indestructible Roller Device or CIRD. Each roller was mounted on a swinging arm, the idea being that when it detonated a mine the arm was hurled up and over its axis in a forward direction and was then forced back into a trailing

36 *A Sherman Crab flailing on a beach in Norfolk. In practice flailing on sand was not favoured since the resulting crater proved to be an obstacle in its own right on a crowded beach.*

37 *The Canadian Indestructible Roller Device fitted to a Sherman tank. Although it was thoroughly tested, even after the war, there is no record of it being used in action.*

mode by the progress of the tank. The CIRD was, therefore, essentially a reconnaissance device that could proceed at normal speed and detect mines without endangering the crews or wrecking a tank. Although the apparatus was available for D-Day and apparently shipped across the Channel, there is no evidence of its use. Most of the other designs by 79th Armoured or the OAC were not adopted at all.

As D-Day approached the initial training gave way to operational trials of a more general nature. Since realism was the keynote it was essential for all the elements to practise as a team and at the same time they needed to carry out live firing trials. The ideal site was found at Linney Head in South Wales and this was wrested from the RAF in the summer of 1943 for collective training. Once again replicas of known German defence works were built and the various elements of the division began to assemble. Down from Cumberland came the CDLs and across from Suffolk the AVREs rolled in. The lonely headland echoed to the sharp crack of 75s and the crump of Petards. The 79th Armoured Division was sharpening its claws.

30

38 *The problem of the blue clay: this Churchill Mark IV is sinking fast while an armoured bulldozer and two Sherman Beach Armoured Vehicles try to pull it out.*

Then all at once there was a new problem. The exact region for the projected landing having been established it became necessary to take a closer look at the beaches. It required a cold-blooded sort of courage to paddle ashore at night on an enemy-held coast and make a close examination of the beach to provide the assault force with the most detailed information, but it was done. One thing these furtive visitors discovered was a geological feature of some beaches that made them a deathtrap for heavy armoured vehicles. In places the sand lightly covered patches of soft blue clay which could disable a tank as effectively as any mine so, with the projected landing a matter of weeks away, there was an urgent need to overcome the problem. A quick search detected similar deposits on the beach at Brancaster Bay on the north Norfolk coast. Immediately another wing of the division established itself there and set to work. Their answer was the Bobbin, a development of the primitive

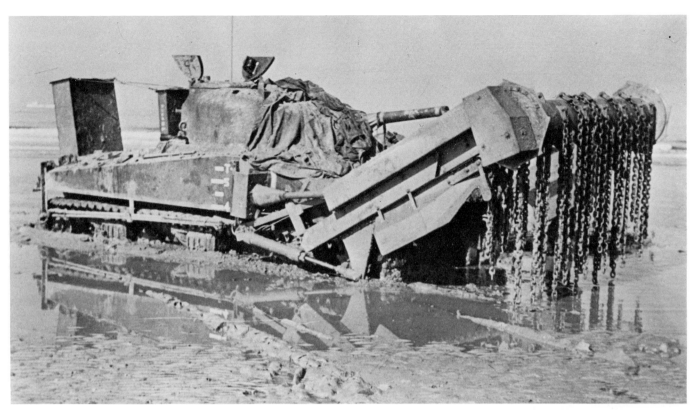

39 *A Crab trapped in blue clay.*

40 *An early version of the Bobbin device demonstrates its ability to operate over barbed wire during trials.*

41 *A Bobbin Mark I drops the last portion of its carpet on the sand at Brancaster Bay.*

42 *A Churchill Mark IV gun tank demonstrates the Bobbin apparatus at Brancaster Bay. This Mark II version is fitted with spikes to locate the matting in line with the tracks.*

device fitted to some Churchills at Dieppe. A framework was designed which fitted to the standard AVRE fittings and from which was suspended a large roll of coir matting strengthened by crosspieces of scaffolding tube. This was laid over the fluid clay by the simple expedient of dropping the end beneath the tracks of the tank, which moved forward unwinding the coil and pressing it down as it went. It didn't last very long once a few tanks had been across it, but it was sufficient for the initial assault and once the beaches were clear a more substantial track of perforated steel plates was laid by hand to replace it.

Another problem was solved with the Bullshorn Plough. It was discovered that, effective as it was, the flail was a liability on soft sand. Detonated mines blew large craters in the beach which became obstacles in their own right, the only reasonable alternative was to lift them. This was achieved by reviving another pre-war idea, the mine-clearing plough, and the OAC had already tested some prototypes based on the Churchill. In its final form the Bullshorn consisted of a pair of skids and wicked looking ploughshares on a subframe extending in front of the tank. On the beach the plough was lowered and pushed through the sand, turning up the mines and pushing them aside to be rendered safe by the sappers.

43 *The Bullshorn Plough attachment on a Churchill IV during trials in Norfolk. Mines were lifted and turned aside by the blade to be rendered safe later.*

Now at last all that could be done was done, the division could field an effective answer to every imaginable problem and there were well-trained crews ready to defeat any obstacle that Rommel could devise. Behind them an enormous army was poised to follow them into France, ahead of them lay the enemy and between the two the English Channel. The vessels that were to carry the armour to France, the Landing Craft Tanks, were designed to carry ordinary fighting tanks not encumbered with a variety of awkward attachments. It, therefore, became necessary to carry out a series of loading trials that would ensure a safe voyage and successful landing. Each craft (except those carrying DD tanks) would load a mixed team of vehicles chosen to suit a specific landing point and much juggling was required to get them aboard and stowed in the correct order. The Royal Navy imposed further limitations since it was essential that the odd mixture should not upset the trim of a particular vessel. The Navy disliked the SBG most of all. A shallow-draught tank-landing craft is very vulnerable to a beam wind and the vast bridge, sticking up in the air, acted like a sail, forever trying to push the ship off course. SBGs were therefore always stowed aft, close to the ship's bridge, in order to minimize the effect. The fascine presented the usual problem of visibility while the Crab, with its projecting booms, was very difficult to manoeuvre through the bow without destroying small fittings like fire buckets. The Bullshorn Plough would ground on the angle between the ramp and the beach while Bobbins and ARKS

44 *Landing practice: two Sherman Crabs and a Churchill AVRE reverse aboard an LCT.*

45 *A Crab making for the beach through the shallows after disembarking from an LCT.*

presented problems of their own. For these and other difficulties to be looked into a selection of specialized vehicles was sent down to the Combined Operations Experimental Establishment (COXE) at Westward Ho! in North Devon where landing craft of the British Mark IV and American Mark V types were systematically loaded and unloaded until all the problems had been ironed out. The longer and wider British version was preferred since it was easier for the tanks to line themselves up with the ramp before disembarking, but both types were used.

A fully laden landing-craft draws about 1.20 metres (4 feet) which means that a dry landing is impossible. A rising tide and a choppy sea can increase the depth of water at the bow to 1.50 metres (5 feet) or more so it became essential to prepare the tanks for temporary operation in the shallows. Measures for doing this were also developed at COXE.

46 *Looking down on an SBG and Bobbin on the beach at Westward Ho! Notice the deep-wading fittings and waterproof covering on the nearest tank.*

47 *Landing craft loading trials with an LCT (5). In the foreground is a Churchill III with an SBG, beyond it a Churchill IV with a framework to represent a demolition device and further back an AVRE with a fascine.*

48 *AVREs with fascines and an SBG on the deck of an LCT. The pipe in the centre is a section of Snake mine-clearing equipment.*

49 *A Churchill AVRE with its fascine in place eases through the bow of an LCT (4).*

Small orifices and gaps, turret rings and hatches, were sealed with a mastic compound and covered with waterproof sheeting while engine air intakes and exhausts were funnelled into vertical trunking well above water level. This material was rapidly discarded on landing, often with the aid of a small explosive charge, and the tank was at once ready for action. This deep wading equipment was applied for operation in up to 1.8 metres (6 feet) of water and special 'pack-flat' kits were supplied for all types of tank.

The trials were complete, the training was over and the date for the invasion had been fixed. Roads, railways and sea lanes to the south of England were jammed to capacity as the allied armies assembled. Craft were loaded, crews were briefed and all awaited the announcement from Southwick House, Eisenhower's Headquarters near Portsmouth, that would set the whole thing in motion. The 79th Armoured Division would soon be in action, for the very first time, on the Normandy beaches.

4 D-Day: Porpoises and Caterpillars

The allied landing in Normandy, codenamed Overlord, began on the morning of 6 June 1944. Strong winds and low cloud created conditions that were less than ideal, but they also served to throw the Germans off their guard. To detail all the actions of the 79th Armoured Division on this day alone would be a mammoth task far beyond the scope of this book, so in an effort to do it some justice we will look at a series of individual incidents that illustrate the events and attempt to show how examples of the various types of equipment so far described coped with their tasks. In order to preserve the sense of authenticity the chosen actions will be based on accounts in the original divisional history.

Among the DD tanks those of the 13/18th Hussars are selected since they, above all, illustrate the true function of the type. The landing craft carrying them hove to nearly 5 kilometres (3 miles) from the shore. Forty Shermans launched into the choppy sea, formed up and headed in, but the strong cross-current and the steep waves slowed them down until they were gradually overtaken by other craft. Soon they were inextricably mixed in with vessels of all shapes and sizes and two DDs were lost when they were run down by LCTs in the confusion. Others foundered and a few were drowned on the water's edge, but finally thirty-three struggled out of the sea to confront the enemy. Their

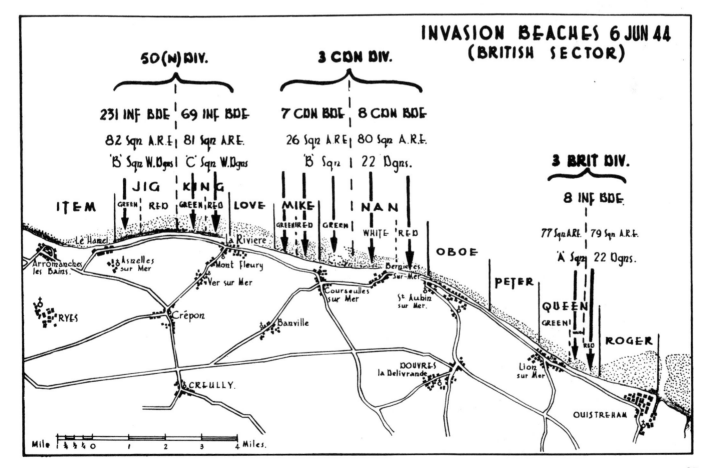

landing area was between Ouistreham and Lion-sur-Mer and the tanks drew very little fire from the enemy as they swam in. For one thing the defenders were badly shaken by the heavy naval bombardment and in any case they were bewildered by the profusion of shipping which presented far more interesting targets than the little canvas boats which were wallowing in the breakers. When the tanks arrived the infantry were already ashore under fierce attack but the DDs dropped their screens and went into action, providing timely support.

50 *D-Day in the British sector. Commandos wade ashore from their LCT while DD Shermans prepare to move off the beach.*

51 *Lion-sur-Mer eight days after D-Day showing the beach strewn with wrecked landing craft, DD tanks and an armoured tractor.*

52 *The view from this German gun position shows a DD tank sharing the beach with a P47D Thunderbolt that force landed on the sand.*

53 *This Sherman DD was another victim of the blue clay. The troops in the background are laying a mesh carpet to enable other vehicles to drive ashore safely.*

54 *On the beach, a bogged Churchill IV AVRE lies beside a spent and discarded Bobbin core.*

55 *The empty core of a discarded Bobbin rests in the dunes at Le Hamel.*

56 *Dried out coasters unload directly into trucks on the beach at Lion-sur-Mer beyond the dump of redundant beach obstacles.*

57 *A successfully laid SBG which has since been bypassed with a steel mesh roadway.*

The beach at Le Hamel was one that featured patches of blue clay. The western most team (No 6) landed a Bobbin equipped AVRE of 82nd Assault Squadron RE, which opened one lane, but a number of vehicles were bogged down in other patches. Once a Bobbin was laid the AVRE discarded the framework and proceeded about its business with the Petard. The enemy held out in the town until midday and the work of other AVREs is notable. One attacked the Sanatorium, a well-fortified local landmark, and effected its surrender with two well-placed Dustbins, it then worked its way round to the rear of an anti-tank gun emplacement which was set alight with another round. Both locations yielded a good crop of prisoners. The surviving AVREs then undertook a variety of beach-clearing tasks, crushing obstacles, recovering other tanks and helping to fill in craters before being summoned inland to support the infantry.

A team of three AVREs on the beach at La Rivière was busily demolishing pillboxes but the infantry were still pinned down by German troops lurking beind the sea-wall, who were lobbing grenades, firing machine guns and generally being a nuisance. The team leader, Captain D.A. King RE, led his and another AVRE in a charge up and over the wall, crashing down a 1.20-metre (4-foot) drop to the road on the far side, thereby putting a stop to the defenders activities.

58 *The crew of a Sherman Crab pause in a burning town.*

The landing area at Courseulles was split in two by the River Seulles and to the east of this two teams landed side by side. First the flails cleared the beach but were disabled in the dunes, the third one in fact became stranded in a flooded crater which turned out to be twelve feet deep. The advance was held up and an AVRE also drowned while attempting to launch its fascine. The placing of another fascine enabled an AVRE with a Small Box Girder Bridge to approach; the bridge was first used to push the fascine off the drowned tank before being lowered to rest on its turret. This precarious assembly remained in use for three hours.

Bullshorn Ploughs were used at Lion-sur-Mer but the Crabs were everywhere. Owing to the delay in landing DDs the mine-sweeping Shermans often found themselves the only effective fire support available for the infantry and at least one, at La Rivière, knocked out an 88mm gun. At Le Hamel a Crab under the command of Sergeant Lindsay flailed its way off the beach and up to the main road, where it turned right and set off for town. The place was found to be heavily defended but Lindsay had a job to do on the other side of town so he carried on along the main street, flailing and firing by turns until he was through. His tank was then hit and knocked out before he could start work on clearing another minefield.

59 *This Churchill AVRE lies abandoned after a mishap on the beach at Le Hamel. It provides an excellent view of the deep-wading attachments to the air intakes and exhausts.*

60 *A Sherman DD towing a Porpoise raft. Half-loaded with ammunition, the raft would float behind the tank.*

Invidious as these selections may be in view of the many courageous acts performed on that momentous day, they serve to illustrate the ingenuity of the 79th Armoured Division and go some way to explain why it was that the British beaches were cleared so swiftly that by evening a salient 32 kilometres (20 miles) wide and in places as much as 13 kilometres (8 miles) deep was secured. Much was also due to effective air superiority and to the fact that the Germans, in failing to appreciate the significance of the landings, refused to commit their Panzer Divisions to counter-attack the beachhead at the crucial time. Comparisons are often drawn between the events on the British and American beaches on D-Day but conclusions must necessarily be guarded for want of proof. Despite a penchant for mechanical ingenuity, the United States Army chose not to rely on specialized armour, except for the DD tanks and the casualties among their engineer troops seem comparable in number to those at Dieppe, but to say that this difference in fortune was due entirely to this factor is perhaps to overstate the case.

Two other devices from the inventory of the 79th Armoured Division played their parts on D-Day and deserve to be mentioned. They made material contributions to success although they lack the glamour of the Funnies. One was Porpoise, a waterproof sledge device that was towed ashore

61 *An armoured bulldozer at work on the beach while Shermans land from an LCT (4). This sort of work made the bulldozers particularly vulnerable to mines.*

by some of the tanks. It provided a simple means of landing extra ammunition, being designed to float partially loaded or skid along the bottom when full. The other was the armoured Caterpillar tractor. This appeared in two forms, as a bulldozer for general clearance work under fire and with a specially designed hull which enabled it to operate in a semi-submerged state to rescue stranded vehicles and small landing craft. This version was in effect a junior brother of the larger Sherman Beach Armoured Recovery Vehicle (BARV) which was designed for the same sort of work.

62 *The waterproof armoured tractor could wade to the rim of its hull.*

63 *The waterproof tractor in action, towing a drowned Scammell ashore. A Rhino ferry lands lorries in the background while barrage balloons float over the dunes.*

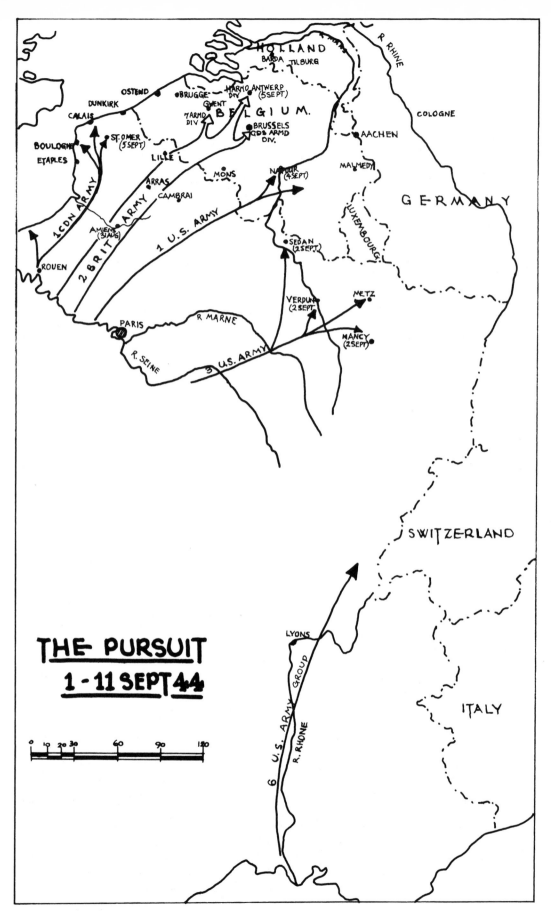

THE PURSUIT
1 - 11 SEPT 44

5 Normandy to Antwerp: Crocodile and Conger

64 *Soldier's eye view of a DD Sherman. The sprocket at the rear end of the tank served as a power take-off to drive the propellors.*

If the 79th had really been what some presumably thought it was, a specialized division for a special day, its story would have ended there, on the beach. But even before the day was over it was obvious that this was only the beginning. Well before dusk, as the Allied forces pushed inland, the cry was heard for Funnies here, Funnies there, until it seemed as if the resources of the division would be exhausted within twenty-four hours. That they were stretched and their limitations tested there is no doubt, but the AVREs in particular were in constant demand, often for tasks that should properly have been done by conventional tanks. Even so they were not to be squandered and the division's liaison officers who accompanied each unit were enjoined to resist demands that would have resulted in misuse and wastage. There were still some tough nuts to crack.

65 *A Churchill ARK Mark II, with its ramps poised for action, moving down a leafy lane in France.*

As the invaders fanned out into the Normandy countryside the specialized armour remained on call to tackle specific problems but their most important tasks at this time centred on the heavily defended Channel ports. These coastal strongholds offered no direct obstacles to the main attack but their importance to the Allies lay in their potential for shortening supply lines from Britain so it was essential that they should be taken as soon as possible. Le Havre fell on 12 September; it was well defended and required the services of almost every element of the division. By this time a new name had joined the lexicon; Crocodile. This apt *nom-de-guerre* was applied to a special version of the Churchill tank designed to carry a flamethrower. It was not the first of its

66 *DD Shermans with their screens removed, halt for a military policeman in Douet.*

67 *A Sherman II DD with its screens removed, passing through Douet followed by a light Stuart.*

kind for as we have seen some earlier examples had landed at Dieppe and almost every tank-producing nation fielded at least one type of mechanized flamethrower. The Crocodile however was by far the best, or worst, depending on which side of it you were fighting. Flame fuel and propellant were stored in a two-wheel armoured trailer while the projector replaced the hull machine gun. With a maximum range of 183 metres (200 yards) it was awe-inspiring and deadly accurate. Its effect was horrendous and the psychological impact alone provided sufficient incentive for surrender in all but the most stubborn cases. The Crocodiles were operated by the 141st RAC. Initially they were not part of the 79th Armoured Division but they came under Hobart's

68 *A Sherman Crab crossing a field bank in Normandy. At this point it was most vulnerable to enemy gunners.*

69 *An assault team forming up for the attack on Le Havre.*

70 *A squadron of Crabs move up while AVREs and infantry wait to advance.*

71 *An experimental flamethrower on a Valentine tank. Flame fuel and propellant are carried in a two-wheel trailer and the projector was mounted at the front in a small turret fitted to the off-side trackguard.*

72 *A Churchill Crocodile gives a flamethrowing demonstration across a railway.*

74 *Troops move aside as Crocodiles of 141 RAC advance during the Le Havre action.*

73 *'Calgary' advances through smouldering evidence of its own destructive power.*

75 *This unhappy AVRE of 284 Squadron fell off the top of a German blockhouse while attempting to outflank a defensive position west of Calais.*

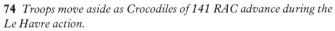

76 *Conger, a Churchill AVRE, towing the modified carrier with its lethal load.*

77 *Looking down into the Conger carrier, showing the pump housing, hose stowage and launcher.*

78 *Conger takes flight and the empty hose curves through the air.*

control in July when it was realized that their peculiar qualities were much in demand and consequently in danger of being misemployed. To avoid this it was essential that they were treated in the same way as the other Funnies, so in they came.

On 14 September a squadron of Crocodiles worked alongside the United States Army during the attack on Brest, while on the 17th the division played a large part in the Canadian attack on Boulogne, which fell on the 21st. During these early months General Hobart divided his time between his home headquarters in Britain and tactical HQ in France, which was under the immediate command of Brigadier (now Major-General) N.W. Duncan. In due course the C.O. was established in France with his division and the two men shared the enormous workload. By the end of the month Cap Gris-Nez and Calais had fallen after equally intense struggles in which the 79th Armoured Division played a prominent part. It was during this action that Conger was used for the first and only time. Conger was a variation on Snake, which itself was an alternative method of breaching minefields. Snake consisted of a series of explosive-filled tubes, connected end to end and pushed by a tank across the minefield. When it was in place the tank withdrew and the charge detonated with sufficient effect to

49

79 *The huge crater blown when a Conger exploded prematurely. The twisted remains of a lorry can be seen but four Churchill AVREs were destroyed as well.*

80 *The crew of this Sherman Crab, not all of whom are in regulation headgear, turn their hands to rural pursuits but retain the bovine connection.*

explode the majority of mines in the immediate vicinity. Its main handicap, besides the difficulty of handling the long pipes, was that it only worked effectively on fairly level ground, whereas Conger, in theory, could cope with all manner of undulations. It consisted of a long coil of hosepipe which was stowed in the gutted hull of a Universal Carrier that was towed into action by an AVRE. At the edge of the minefield the hose was launched at the tail of a rocket to fall over the field while the rear end remained anchored to the carrier. Then came the tricky bit, highly volatile liquid explosive was pumped into the hose to be detonated in the same way as Snake. The result was spectacular and effective when it worked properly but the snag lay in the unstable nature of the explosive, which did not take kindly to being pumped. On one fateful occasion the premature explosion of one of these units completely destroyed four Churchill AVREs and attendant transport, blowing an enormous crater in the field. Although it was earmarked for further development it was never again used in action.

As autumn approached one more great port beckoned, Antwerp, which would be, when captured, the vital point of entry for supplies and reinforcements for the final assault on Germany.

81 *A Crab, with its boom raised to improve forward vision is guided across a Bailey bridge.*

6 Antwerp and Walcheren Buffalo, Weasel and Terrapin

The city of Antwerp lies well inland but has access to the sea via the navigable reaches of the River Scheldt. The 11th Armoured Division, Hobart's previous charge, took it early in September but the harbour facilities remained an unrealized asset since the Germans held a vast area of low-lying land and islands, which controlled the estuary and denied it to Allied shipping. The 79th Armoured Division, with their unique experience of amphibious warfare, had the responsibility of wresting this uninviting terrain from the enemy and opening up the waterway.

Before we take a look at these actions it is essential to introduce three more specialized vehicles that joined the division and made significant contributions to the success of the enterprise. The most important was the Buffalo. This was a generic title bestowed by the British on a series of large amphibians more correctly known as Landing Vehicles Tracked (LVT). They were American machines which had their origins in a prototype developed by a Florida engineer, Donald Roebling. They had been constructed to transport men and materials in the swampy Everglades and came to the attention of the US Marine Corps, who recognized their advantages as ship-to-shore assault craft for the Pacific theatre. None were available for D-Day but four months later they were in service with the British Army for the Scheldt operations. Two types were used, the LVT II, which was a rear-engined model with a central hold, and the LVT IV, which had a front-mounted engine and a hinged ramp that enabled it to transport light vehicles and guns in addition to the more usual payloads of troops or stores. A limited amount of armour was applied to the forward end and Browning machine guns were carried for immediate defence. Despite their size, ground pressure was low, permitting operations in soft mud, and, freeboard being minimal, they maintained a low profile in the water. The tracks were fitted with special scoops to enable them to swim but they were very vulnerable to wear on land and the overall bulk of the machine made it an easy target out of the water. The baby brother of the Buffalo was the Weasel. This was again an American type built by the Studebaker Corporation. As the M29 utility vehicle it had originally been designed for driving over snow, but the M29C was equipped with floatation pontoons front and rear, which turned it into a sort of tracked amphibious Jeep. A single Weasel could carry four men or a load of about 410 kilogrammes (8 cwt), so they had to be used *en masse* to achieve any effect, but their low ground pressure allowed them to penetrate areas which were otherwise inaccessible to mechanical transport. The Buffalos served in the primary assault role, the Weasels did liaison work while the back-up transportation was in charge of the Terrapins.

Few vehicles made an impact on warfare that compared with the redoubtable DUKW. This superb American amphibian was a classic conversion of a six-wheel-drive truck. It was General Hobart's first choice as a field command vehicle and it served its users well from the Pacific to the Mediterranean, from Normandy to the Rhine and long after. It was not without its rivals but the only one to reach production was the Terrapin. This was a Thornycroft design manufactured by Morris-Commercial Motors in 1944. Unlike the DUKW it was a very specialized

82 *Terrapin Mark I, the British answer to the DUKW. The awkward location of the driver is well shown, as are the separate stowage holds.*

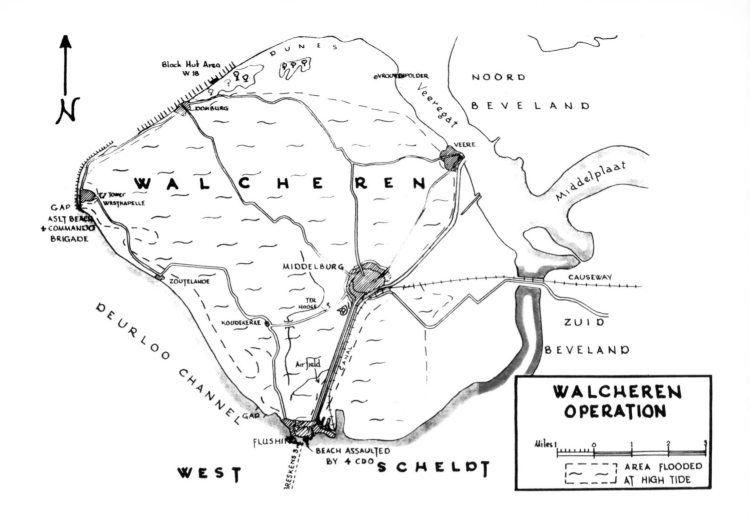

DUNES

Black Hut Area
W 18

VROUWENPOLDER

NOORD
BEVELAND

Veeregat

WALCHEREN

DOMBURG

VEERE

Middelplaat

TV Tower
WESTKAPELLE

GAP
ASLT BEACH
4 COMMANDO
BRIGADE

MIDDELBURG

ZOUTELANDE

CAUSEWAY

ZUID

TER
HOOGE

BEVELAND

KOUDEKERKE

Airfield

CANAL

GAP

FLUSHING

BRESKENS 3½

BEACH ASSAULTED
BY 4 CDO

WEST   SCHELDT

DEURLOO CHANNEL

**WALCHEREN
OPERATION**

Miles 1 ———— 0 ———— 1 ———— 2 ———— 3

- - - - ~ ~ ~   AREA FLOODED
                AT HIGH TIDE

83 *A column of Loyd Carriers, towing anti-tank guns, pass a waiting Crab.*

84 *There are not many smiling faces among the passengers aboard LCT (4) number 789 as she carries her Buffalo towards Walcheren.*

85 *In the anxious moments before landing a group of commandos pose beside a machine-gun.*

86 *A well laden Buffalo aboard an LCT. The special tracks that move it through the water are clearly shown.*

design running on eight wheels. On a hard surface the leading wheels were held clear of the road, only coming into use on uneven ground, as for instance when climbing out of a river. It was equipped with two engines, arranged to drive the wheels on either side so that one steered by slowing down one engine and causing the vehicle to skid round. It had twin propellers and rudders for water-borne work. Despite the fact that it could carry nearly twice the payload of a DUKW, it proved a poor substitute. For some reason the designers chose to station the driver amidships with separate cargo holds fore and aft. This limited loading possibilities and restricted the driver's view. However the supply of DUKWs was not unlimited so some 500 Terrapins were built and they served with 5 Armoured Engineer Regiment RE.

Operations in the Scheldt Estuary began on 8 October with a move to clear the south bank by an amphibious flank attack from Terneuzen. More elements of the division became involved as the attack was pressed westwards to clear the coast as far as Zeebrugge. Meanwhile the town of Terneuzen became the jumping off point for another waterborne assault, this time across the river to clear the South Beveland peninsula. DD tanks appeared again for this operation in charge of the Staffordshire Yeomanry while 11th RTR joined 5 Assault Regiment as a Buffalo-equipped force. The LVT IIs, being awkward things to unload, served as troop carriers only while the IVs handled both troops and supplies. In all these operations the work of the Buffalo did not end with the landing. Once their charges were unloaded they returned with prisoners and wounded to collect a second load.

The key to the Scheldt, however, was the island of Walcheren which dominates the estuary, despite being almost awash at high tide. Naturally the Germans

87 *LCT (4) number 737 disgorges a Crab at Walcheren while, further out, a sister ship launches its Buffalo.*

88 *A Crab struggles ashore from its LCT. Another flail is just approaching the ramp.*

89 *A column of Buffalo wallows in the mud while an armoured D8 bulldozer in the foreground deals with the shore obstacles.*

90 *Weasels and Buffalo coming ashore.*

91 *A Weasel struggles past a stranded AVRE, followed by a Crab. Just visible in the background, another landing craft turns away with an SBG aboard.*

92 *An LVT II amidst the mud and desolation on Walcheren.*

93 *A group of German prisoners shiver in the shallows beside a Sherman Crab in the aftermath of landing.*

appreciated this and it was very well and, as it proved, tenaciously defended. It position at the very mouth of the river made it vulnerable to attack from both river and sea so the operation to clear it was a full-blooded naval and military affair. With typical Dutch ingenuity the island was protected from the worst ravages of the sea by coastal dykes, but the RAF successfully breached these and seriously hampered the defence. The major assault, led by 4 Commando Brigade, landed in the west while a smaller force attacked Flushing in the south. Buffalos were launched from LCTs while Crabs and AVREs in company with armoured bulldozers were delivered direct to the shore. The enemy

were well prepared and the landing craft suffered accordingly. The shoreline was a mud bath which trapped men and machines. The assault began on 1 November and the result hung in the balance for thirty-six hours; it took five more days to clear the island completely.

Antwerp was finally opened to shipping at the end of November and for the remaining months of 1944 79th Armoured Division was involved in a series of operations designed to clear up German resistance west of the Maas. They were involved to a limited degree in the improvised riposte to the great German counter thrust in the Ardennes.

7 Across the Rhine: Kangaroo and Centaur

By early February 1945 allied forces were advancing towards the Rhine. The plan was about two months behind schedule due to the so-called Battle of the Bulge and the mid-winter freeze had thawed leaving large areas of low-lying ground under water, or thick with mud. Much of the region now to be fought over was covered by the dense, gloomy forest of the Reichswald and it included the vaunted Siegfried Line. The coming battles were to involve every element of 79th Armoured Division so far mentioned plus a couple of new ones. The foremost of these was the Kangaroo. This code name was applied to turretless tanks which had been converted to carry eight infantrymen in reasonable security. The tanks chosen for this work were Canadian built Rams, a parallel design to the Sherman, which had otherwise been relegated to training. The British 49th Armoured Personnel Carrier Regiment and the 1st Canadian Armoured Carrier Regiment had joined the division with their vehicles in December. It was now possible to transport infantry in company with the tanks to their mutual advantage, especially in close country like the Reichswald, where the defenders employed the cover to stalk tanks with portable anti-tank weapons of the bazooka type. As soon as such opposition was discovered the infantry would dismount and winkle out the opposition before resuming the advance. The conditions were appalling and casualties high, so it was early March before the Allies finally emerged from the forests and swamps onto the banks of the Rhine itself.

Meanwhile the requirement for specialized armour had expanded. Faced with a river like the Rhine, the division reverted to a number of techniques first adopted for D-Day, but one of the main differences was the nature of the waterway to be crossed. Compared with the relatively firm level beaches of Normandy, the banks of the Rhine were steep and muddy so it became necessary to devise new means of enabling the amphibious vehicles, especially the DD tanks, to climb out. Thus a series of experimental wings were formed to devise new methods of dealing with these problems.

F Wing, based at Gheel in Belgium, tested a series of anti-mine devices to combat the anti-personnel Schu mine, a vicious little weapon that discharged shrapnel at knee level.

94 *Time for a brew up. This SBG-equipped AVRE waits while its crew take a breather.*

95 *Infantrymen clamber aboard their Kangaroo. The tank has been fitted with track grousers to help it through the mud.*

96 *A column of Kangaroos on the road, their passengers protected from everything but the rain.*

98 *Rodent was a device for clearing Schu mines, developed by F Wing and attached to an M29 Weasel.*

97 *The leading Crab in this column has lost its flail boom but continues to serve as a gun tank until repairs can be effected. Notice how the rotors on the following tanks have been wrapped in canvas for long-distance travel.*

99 *Flo is an M29 Weasel being used to test another minesweeping device called Suggy.*

100 *F Wing demonstrates its version of the Bobbin which featured a larger, wider carpet.*

101 *F Wing had a hand in the design of the Centaur Dozer but production was undertaken in Britain.*

The lightweight Weasels were used as carriers for two or three such contraptions, none of which were used, while attempts were made, unsuccessfully as it turned out, to employ Crocodiles to explode mines with flame. The spectacular Canadian Indestructible Roller device was tested again as was a safer variation of Conger, called Tapeworm. AVREs were adapted to lay carpets without the added complication of the Bobbin attachment and the Small Box Girder Bridge was modified to make it easier to

transport. The most effective contribution made by F Wing was the tank dozer which was simply a turretless Centaur cruiser tank with a large blade for filling craters and shifting rubble. These gradually replaced the armoured D8 bull-dozers since they were more mobile and better protected. They did not come into their own until after the Rhine crossing when they were used to force new paths through devastated German towns.

102 *Inland an armoured D8 clears a wrecked vehicle from the roadway.*

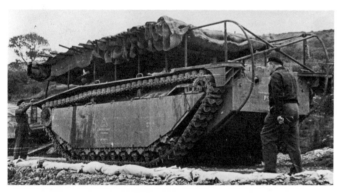

103 *G Wing converted some Buffalo to carry and lay carpets on river banks to assist DD tanks climbing ashore. This type used a mat made of wooden strips joined by cable.*

104 *An alternative version employed a large sheet of canvas stiffened with rods.*

G Wing, which was established on the banks of the Maas, dealt with the problems of large-scale river crossing. Their most effective device took the form of a carpet of logs, connected by wire, which was supported on rails on a Buffalo. The amphibian laid its mat as it climbed ashore on the farther bank and this provided a firm grip for the DD tanks to climb over. G Wing also trained crews for the class 30/60 rafts, which were to act as tank ferries along with small landing craft until proper bridges had been established.

H Wing, at Nijmegen, also dealt in rafting; tanks parked on the river bank served as anchoring points for the cable while the rafts were hauled across the river by RAF barrage balloon winch lorries.

J Wing, located close to H at Waal, specialized in navigation techniques. The broad waters of the Rhine presented a challenge to DD tanks and Buffalo alike when it came to steering a course for a specific point on the opposite bank. The difficulties would be increased at night or in a smoke screen so a variety of devices involving compasses, radio direction keeping and illuminated beacons were perfected.

105 *During trials on the Meuse a DD tank prepares to test the carpet which has been laid on the far bank.*

106 *A Valentine Archer boards a raft during trials. The RAF winch lorry is seen on the left with the Churchill anchor tank on the right.*

107 *Gutted Universal Carriers were used as supply trailers. This one, being towed by a Crocodile contains bridging materials.*

108 *Infantry practice boarding a Buffalo under the watchful eye of the crew. Some are wearing life preservers.*

109 *Loading a Jeep into a Buffalo. This LVT IV has small covers added to the Browning machine-gun mounts, and a smoke discharger on the right.*

110 *Sherman DD tanks waiting for the order to move up for the Rhine crossing.*

111 *The LVT IV Buffalo was quite capable of carrying a Universal Carrier and a number crossed the Rhine in this way.*

112 *A column of Buffalo moving up in the dusk. The leading vehicle, in addition to its two Browning machine guns, carries a 20mm Polsten cannon, another fixture devised by the 79th Armoured Division.*

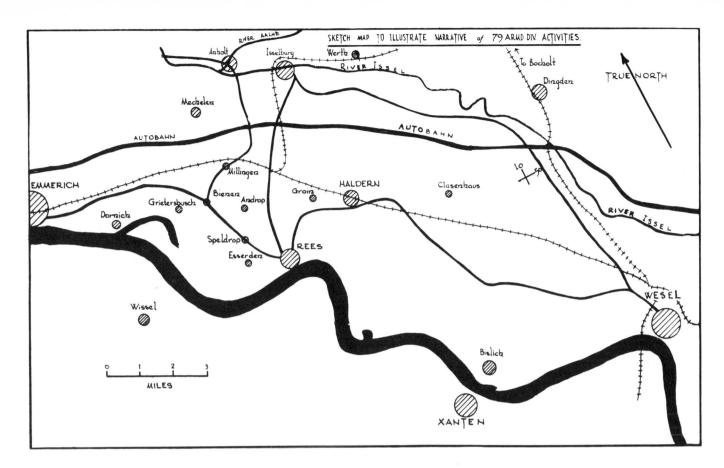

The date of the Rhine crossing was decreed as 23 March and the British and Commonwealth forces operated on a two-division front, some 16 kilometres (ten miles) as the crow flies between Rees and Wesel. Bombing in the early evening gave way to an enormous bombardment with the first Buffalo crossing in its wake. Unlike the Atlantic Wall, the eastern bank of the Rhine was not finished with concrete emplacements or mines so AVREs and Crabs were not urgently required, instead the task fell to the Buffalo, acting as personnel carriers supported by DD tanks until the rafts could be prepared. It took a Buffalo about four minutes to make the crossing and they were used far more than hitherto as carriers to take the infantry on to the fighting

113 *LVT IV Buffalo carrying Jeep ambulances move up to the Rhine.*

114 *Buffalo taking the plunge. The vehicle on the left shows the special scoop-shaped tracks adapted for water propulsion.*

115 *Buffalo amphibians make the four-minute crossing of the Rhine in the last evening light.*

line as it moved away from the river. It took three days to secure the bridgehead and construct proper bridges against strong opposition but on 26 March six Buffalo of B Squadron 11th RTR had the honour of transporting an exalted party including the Prime Minister and senior army commanders (including General Hobart) across the river.

The Rhine crossing also saw the action debut of the CDL tanks, although not in their intended role. Despite lengthy and secretive training they had so far remained on the sidelines, but on the night of the 24th B Squadron 49th RTR forsook its Kangaroos in favour of its original equipment

when the modified Grants trundled up to the river bank. Their initial task was to provide illumination to aid the Buffalo in the vicinity of Rees, where they drew a lot of enemy fire and loud curses from allied units stationed nearby. On subsequent nights the lights were used to scan the river for mines and enemy demolition teams intent on wrecking the bridges. Any suspicious object which was caught in the beam was treated to a hail of gunfire. If any attempts were made to sabotage the crossings they certainly failed.

116 *A Buffalo emerging from the river. Driver and co-driver have their hatches open.*

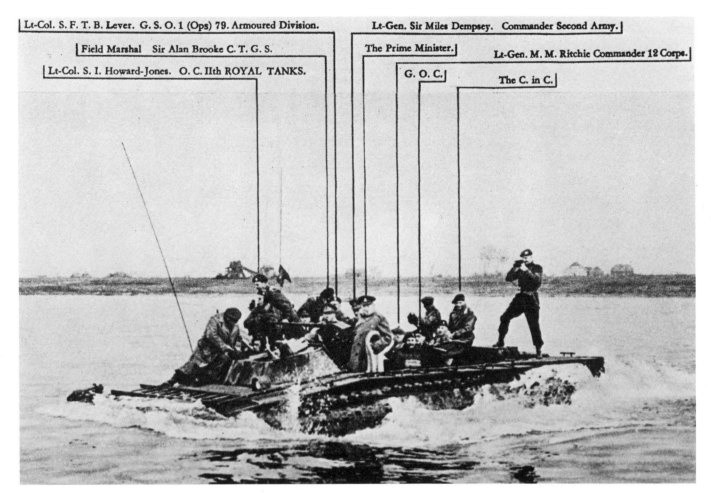

Lt-Col. S. F. T. B. Lever. G. S. O. 1 (Ops) 79. Armoured Division.

Field Marshal Sir Alan Brooke C. T. G. S.

Lt-Col. S. I. Howard-Jones. O. C. IIth ROYAL TANKS.

Lt-Gen. Sir Miles Dempsey. Commander Second Army.

The Prime Minister.

Lt-Gen. M. M. Ritchie Commander 12 Corps.

G. O. C.

The C. in C.

117 *A Buffalo of 11 RTR with a distinguished passenger list. Winston Churchill is prominent, with his life jacket under his arm. The GOC is, of course, General Hobart and the C-in-C Montgomery.*

118 *A Churchill AVRE makes the crossing on a raft.*

119 *A Sherman DD tanks passes a Hamilcar glider on the west bank. The glider carried a light tank which, it appears, has driven out while the nose door was still shut.*

120 *The crew of a Universal Carrier watch as a DD Sherman moves by.*

121 *An excellent view of a fully stowed Crab on the road. Visible at the rear are the station-keeping lights, spare flail chains in their rack and the sloping box which dispenses illuminated pegs to mark the cleared lane through a minefield.*

122 *Churchill AVRE IVs of 617 Assault Squadron RE entering Geilenkerken.*

123 *An AVRE on the road. The hull fittings for special attachments are visible near the front.*

With the Rhine behind them the Allied armies in the west had five more weeks of war to wage. It was a curious mixture of fanatical defence and mass surrender, impressions ranged from horror at the discovery of extermination camps, to awe when the hulks of the huge Maus tanks were found at Meppen. The 79th was everywhere, in Buffalo amidst the floods in Holland, in Kangaroos and AVREs, Crabs and Crocodiles and Centaurs in the ruined cities. The United States 9th Army received unstinting aid from flamethrowers and flails while the pressure was maintained right through to 4 May, when Field-Marshal Montgomery witnessed the surrender by a German delegation on Lüneberg Heath.

The end of the war in Europe caught one spectacular new device before it could be used in action. This was Great Eastern, a turretless Churchill tank with strengthened suspension that carried an impressive ramp structure intended to provide a crossing point for tanks faced with high walls and similar obstacles. Once in place, groups of rockets were fired which flung the extension ramps clear over the wall in a huge arc. Tanks could then climb up the sloping back of the tank, across the wall and down the unfolded ramp on the other side. One of the first examples caught up with Brigadier Duncan in Holland, where he used it as a gigantic firework for newly liberated Dutch folk.

124 *A Churchill gun tank crosses the ramp of Great Eastern during the demonstration at Deventer.*

8 The Specialized Armour Development Establishment

The wartime activities of the 79th Armoured Division ceased when Germany capitulated; they never went to the Far East. Similar equipment was employed in the war against Japan, the Americans making extensive use of amphibians in the island campaigns and the Australian Army developing what they called Circus Equipment, based on the Matilda, which mirrored much of what had been used in Europe.

The return of peace separates the citizen soldier from his professional counterpart in that the former discards his uniform as soon as possible while the latter carries on with his duty. So it was with Hobart; he saw the post-war world as another challenge and his faith in the peculiar services of specialized armour encouraged him to continue its development. With War Office approval he established a new organization at Woodbridge in Suffolk, with an amphibious wing at Gosport in Hampshire which was known as the Specialized Armour Development Establishment, SADE. It lasted for six years. The dual tasks were to improve existing equipment and develop new ideas.

Despite the fact that it was hardly used during the war, the CDL idea was continued. An automatic carbon-feed system was designed to obviate the need for manual replacement and a more compact form of light was produced for fitting to the turret of the new Centurion tank. This had the advantage of retaining the tank's main armament so that special types of tanks were not required. An alternative system using mercury vapour lights was also tested on a Cromwell.

The Churchill Crocodile, which again saw service in Korea, was modified in various details. The internal controls for the flame projector were improved and the pressure system for fuel delivery was changed to eliminate leakage which had bedevilled the wartime models. The Crocodile trailer was fitted with floatation apparatus which permitted it to be towed by a DD tank and a prototype Centurion Crocodile appeared. However the trend was towards self-contained tank flamethrowers instead of trailers so no further versions of Crocodile were made.

The Sherman Crab had more than vindicated its potential and by the end of the war a Mark II version, which was better able to follow ground contours, had been evolved. SADE experimented with smaller diameter rotor drums to reduce the incidence of damage by blast and a reduction gearbox was inserted into the rotor drive on a Mark II in order to reduce the flailing rate. This was in answer to a German practice of linking pairs of mines as an antidote to

125 *Topee was a device applied to the Sherman DD for operations in the Far East. The vulnerable screen was stowed behind a protective casing, which saved it from damage in heavily wooded country.*

126 *Topee with the floatation screen erected.*

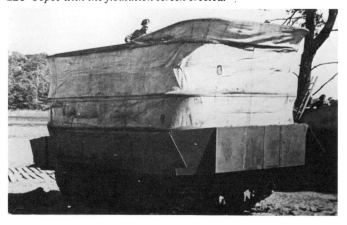

127 *Twelve ATOG rockets fitted on a Churchill IV as part of the SADE minesweeping experiments.*

Crab. The problem of station keeping between flail tanks in action was investigated in a variety of ways including the unlikely expedient of chaining two tanks together; needless to say, this was not a solution that worked very well. Other minesweeping options were tried using rockets and jets. The rockets, 5-inch ATOG type, of the kind used for assisted take-off on aircraft, were mounted at the front of a tank. Starting with single and triple mountings, the theme was extended until a Mark IV Churchill appeared with no less

than twelve of them on an angled framework. They could clear mines alright but they burned out too quickly and further development was not considered worthwhile. A turretless Valentine was used for the jet engine tests. The unit employed was a W2/700 gas turbine which was mounted on the nose of the tank at an angle, pointing downwards. It was worked up to full revs at which time the tank moved slowly forwards against the mines. The blast from the jet carved a shallow trench in the soil and the

128 *SADE spectacular; the mine-clearing jet testbed on an old Valentine hull.*

130 *G Wing had already adapted Buffalo to carry guns but after the war SADE did a more thorough job, as this view shows. An LVT IV is fitted with ramps to load and transport a 17 pounder anti-tank gun.*

129 *Gin-and-It; Straussler's complicated mat-laying device for the DD during initial trials on the Trent.*

offending mine was thrown some 8 metres (9 yards) without detonating. However, results varied to such an extent that this scheme, too, was soon abandoned.

Numerous detail improvements were also made to the DD Sherman. Special drivers' periscopes were tried and remote control machine guns were mounted on the rim of the screen. The most impressive devices, however, were connected with the beaching trials. These were a continuation of the experiments conducted on the Maas. Two different schemes were examined. One was another Straussler idea called Gin-and-It, suggesting that it was conceived in a bar! It consisted of a complicated arrangement of canvas on tubular metal frames which extended from the bow of the tank upon landing and formed a solid path across the mud. An even more spectacular solution was rocket egress. It involved further use of the ATOG rockets mounted, eight a side, on the tank. If it became stuck in the shallows, the rockets were fired and, in

131 *Sea Serpent was a flamethrowing device mounted on an LVT IV. It is shown during SADE trials at Studland Bay.*

theory at least, the tank leapt ashore. The results were reasonably successful, unlike the Gin-and-It, which failed every time, but somewhat overawing to on-lookers due to the amount of flame which enveloped the tank at the critical moment. On dry land ATOG was tested for unditching and an unmanned Universal Carrier did some spectacular rocket-assisted departures from a muddy hole.

Returning to the DDs it is interesting to note that the Kangaroo idea was developed to the extent that a Sherman DD Kangaroo was built, or at least converted from a redundant service tank. The idea was eminently practical but never developed. At the same time an American amphibious device, the T12 system, was tested. This employed vast rubber pontoons attached to the sides of the tank. The main advantage was the fact that the tank could fire while afloat, but it was impossible to launch it from an LCT because of the great width. The American LVT and its British equivalent were tested with a variety of fittings, including a flame-throwing system called Sea Serpent.

The Wartime Churchill AVRE was gradually replaced in service by a new version based on the Mark VII, mounting a 6.5 inch demolition gun, while improved types of fascine, using lighter materials, were developed and at least one tank was fitted with a fascine-launching platform above the turret.

Improved versions of the ARK appeared with longer, wider ramps, and one version, known as Woodlark, launched its ramps by rocket like the Great Eastern.

Even an august body like SADE was not entirely free from flights of fancy – quite literally, in one case. This was the famous gap-jumping tank, which was designed to fly across impassable obstacles. The object was to lift the tank bodily into the air by means of rockets. This device, tested first on a carrier and subsequently on another turretless Valentine,

132 *Burmark, as its name implies, was an ARK device prepared for use in the Far East. It was mounted on a Valentine tank chassis.*

133 *Woodlark was a rocket launched ARK developed by SADE. It is being tested by a standard Churchill Mark VII.*

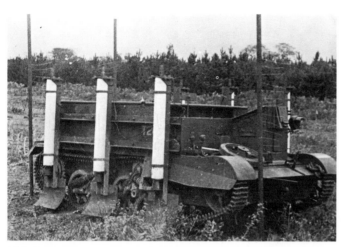

134 *SADE spectacular: the flying carrier before launching.*

(top right)

135 *SADE disaster: the same carrier in its usual post-flight attitude.*

consisted of a battery of rockets which were fired together to catapult the tank through the air. No problem was encountered in lifting the vehicle off the ground; the difficulty was getting it to land the same way up. Quite what happened in the air was never clear since the tank was invisible in a cloud of smoke, but despite a series of tests the stability problem was never solved.

The Specialized Armour Development Establishment, which later became known as the Specialized Armour Establishment (SAE), lasted until 1951. Its final report, the cover of which still sported the famous bull's-head device, revealed the great range of ideas that it had been connected with, from prosaic improvements in rapid refuelling to the advanced concept of using television for reconnaissance purposes. But it also records a trend to deviation that exceeded its brief. On one level it got involved in the user trials of a new quarter ton truck called the Land Rover which, with suitable modifications, it reckoned an adequate substitute for the Jeep! On quite another level it undertook a far-reaching assessment of the modern fighting tank itself.

Arguing that recent increases in size and weight would in time prove prohibitive, the SAE produced a design and a full-sized wooden mock-up of a revolutionary light tank which took advantage of the most up-to-date, indeed futuristic, developments in engine and weapon design coupled with ingenious new proposals for crew stations. This move brought it into competition and conflict with the official War Office body charged with such matters, which no doubt hastened its closure. The mantle of its more legitimate work passed to the 7th Royal Tank Regiment at Bovington, while General Hobart retired.

History was bound to repeat itself. The Centurion was the last British tank to appear in a variety of specialized versions including AVRE, ARK and DD. True, some of its functions have been taken over by the versatile Combat Engineer Tractor, but others have vanished altogether, although the memory lingers on and the fighting in the Falkland Islands has aroused new interest in mechanical minesweeping.

136 *An early Series I Landrover makes its way into a swamp during comparative trials with the Jeep in the background.*

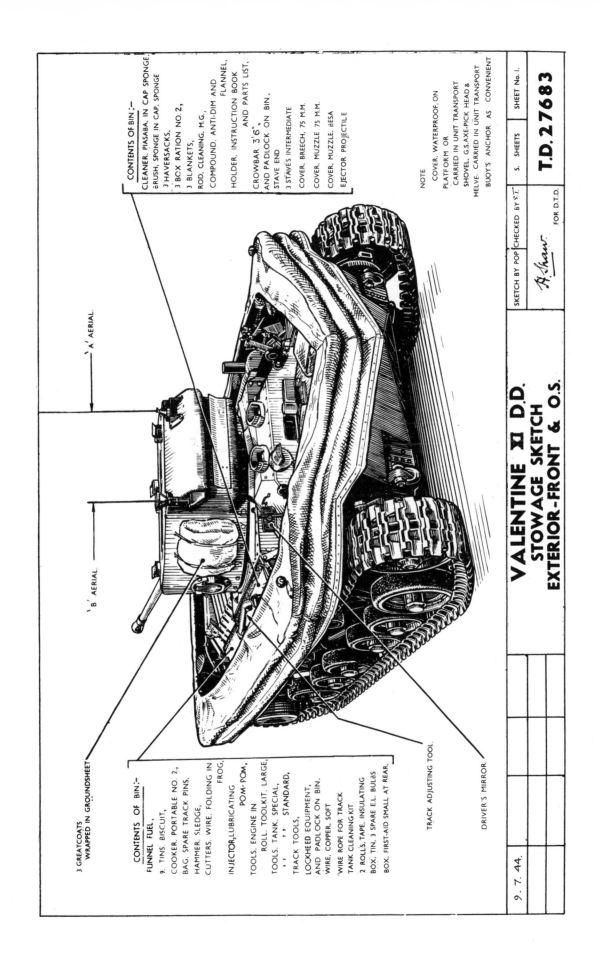

CONTENTS OF BIN:-
CLEANER. PIASABA, IN CAP. SPONGE.
BRUSH, SPONGE IN CAP. SPONGE
3 HAVERSACKS,
3 BCX RATION NO. 2,
3 BLANKETS,
ROD, CLEANING, M.G.,
COMPOUND, ANTI-DIM AND
                    FLANNEL,
HOLDER, INSTRUCTION BOOK
            AND PARTS LIST,
CROWBAR. 3'6",
AND PADLOCK ON BIN.
STAVE END
3 STAVES INTERMEDIATE
COVER, BREECH, 75 M.M.
COVER, MUZZLE 75 M.M.
COVER, MUZZLE, BESA
EJECTOR PROJECTILE

NOTE
COVER, WATERPROOF, ON
PLATFORM OR
CARRIED IN UNIT TRANSPORT
SHOVEL. G.S.AXE-PICK HEAD &
HELVE. CARRIED IN UNIT TRANSPORT
BUOY'S ANCHOR AS CONVENIENT

'A' AERIAL.

'B' AERIAL.

3 GREATCOATS
WRAPPED IN GROUNDSHEET

CONTENTS OF BIN:-
FUNNEL FUEL,
9. TINS. BISCUIT,
COOKER. PORTABLE NO. 2,
BAG. SPARE TRACK PINS,
HAMMER, SLEDGE,
CUTTERS. WIRE. FOLDING IN
                    FROG,
INJECTOR, LUBRICATING
                POM-POM,
TOOLS, ENGINE IN
ROLL. TOOLKIT. LARGE,
TOOLS. TANK. SPECIAL,
  "   "   STANDARD,
TRACK TOOLS,
LOCKHEED EQUIPMENT,
AND PADLOCK ON BIN.
WIRE, COPPER, SOFT
'WIRE ROPE FOR TRACK
TANK CLEANING KIT
2 ROLLS, TAPE, INSULATING
BOX. TIN, 3 SPARE E.L. BULBS
BOX. FIRST-AID SMALL AT REAR.

TRACK ADJUSTING TOOL.

DRIVER'S MIRROR.

VALENTINE XI D.D.
STOWAGE SKETCH
EXTERIOR-FRONT & O.S.

SKETCH BY POP	CHECKED BY S.T.	SHEET No. I.
	A. Shaw FOR D.T.D.	

9. 7. 44.	S. SHEETS	**T.D.27683**

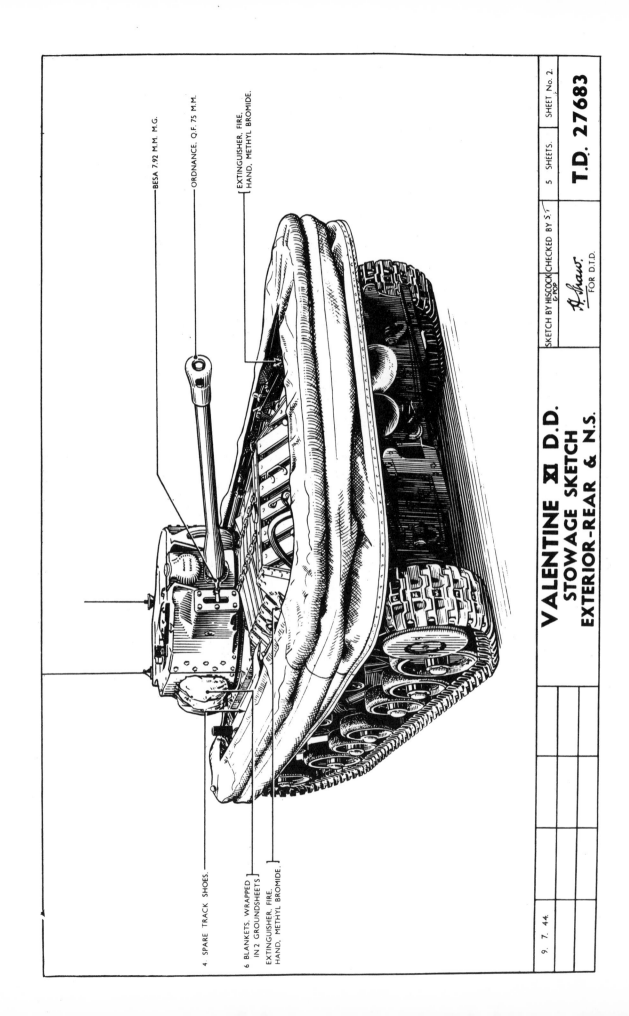

BESA 7.92 M.M. M.G.

ORDNANCE. Q.F. 75 M.M.

EXTINGUISHER, FIRE,
HAND, METHYL BROMIDE.

4 SPARE TRACK SHOES.

6 BLANKETS, WRAPPED
IN 2 GROUNDSHEETS

EXTINGUISHER, FIRE,
HAND, METHYL BROMIDE.

VALENTINE XI D.D.
STOWAGE SKETCH
EXTERIOR-REAR & N.S.

SKETCH BY HISCOCK
& POP

CHECKED BY S.I.

R. Shaw.
FOR D.I.D.

5 SHEETS.   SHEET No. 2.

T.D. 27683

9. 7. 44.

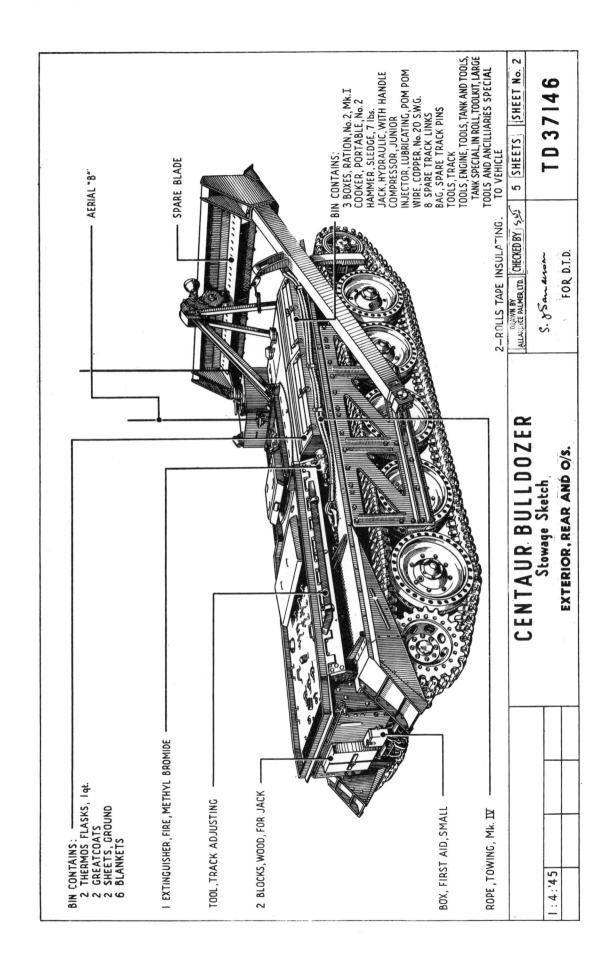

AERIAL "B"

SPARE BLADE

BIN CONTAINS:
2 THERMOS FLASKS, 1qt.
2 GREATCOATS
2 SHEETS, GROUND
6 BLANKETS

1 EXTINGUISHER, FIRE, METHYL BROMIDE

TOOL, TRACK ADJUSTING

2 BLOCKS, WOOD, FOR JACK

BOX, FIRST AID, SMALL

ROPE, TOWING, Mk. IV

BIN CONTAINS:
3 BOXES, RATION, No. 2, Mk. I
COOKER, PORTABLE, No. 2
HAMMER, SLEDGE, 7 lbs.
JACK, HYDRAULIC, WITH HANDLE
COMPRESSOR, JUNIOR
INJECTOR, LUBRICATING, POM POM
WIRE, COPPER, No. 20 S.W.G.
8 SPARE TRACK LINKS
BAG, SPARE TRACK PINS
TOOLS, TRACK
TOOLS, ENGINE, TOOLS, TANK AND TOOLS,
TANK SPECIAL, IN ROLL, TOOLKIT, LARGE
TOOLS AND ANCILLIARIES SPECIAL
TO VEHICLE

2-ROLLS TAPE INSULATING.

CENTAUR BULLDOZER
Stowage Sketch.

EXTERIOR, REAR AND O/S.

1 : 4 : '45

DRAWN BY ALLANDICE PALMER LTD.	CHECKED BY بر	5 SHEETS	SHEET No. 2
S. Sanderson			
FOR D.I.D.			**TD 37146**

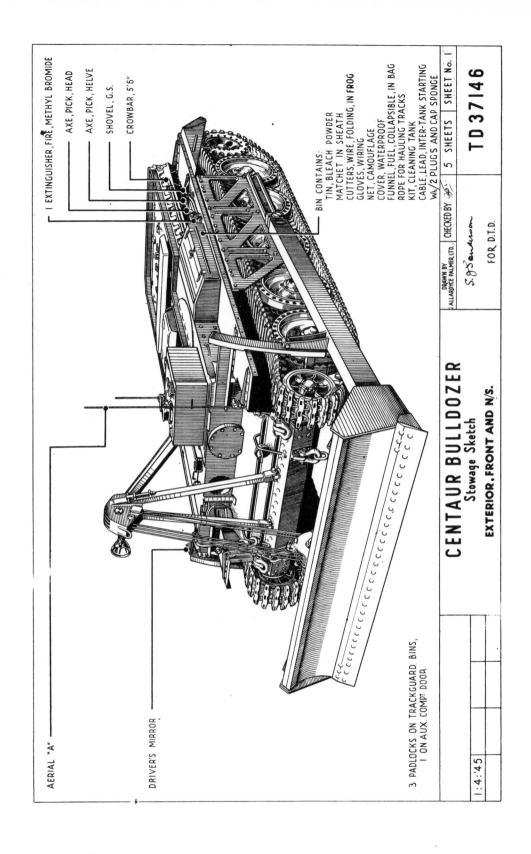

AERIAL "A"

DRIVER'S MIRROR

3 PADLOCKS ON TRACKGUARD BINS,
1 ON AUX. COMP.^T DOOR

1 EXTINGUISHER, FIRE, METHYL BROMIDE

AXE, PICK, HEAD

AXE, PICK, HELVE

SHOVEL, G.S.

CROWBAR, 5'6"

BIN CONTAINS:
TIN, BLEACH POWDER
MATCHET IN SHEATH
CUTTERS, WIRE, FOLDING, IN FROG
GLOVES, WIRING
NET, CAMOUFLAGE
COVER, WATERPROOF
FUNNEL, FUEL, COLLAPSIBLE, IN BAG
ROPE FOR HAULING TRACKS
KIT, CLEANING TANK
CABLE, LEAD, INTER-TANK STARTING
W.2 PLUGS AND CAP SPONGE

CENTAUR BULLDOZER
Stowage Sketch
EXTERIOR, FRONT AND N/S.

1:4:45			DRAWN BY ALLARDYCE PALMER, LTD.	CHECKED BY S. Henderson FOR D.T.D.	5 SHEETS	SHEET No. 1
					TD37146	

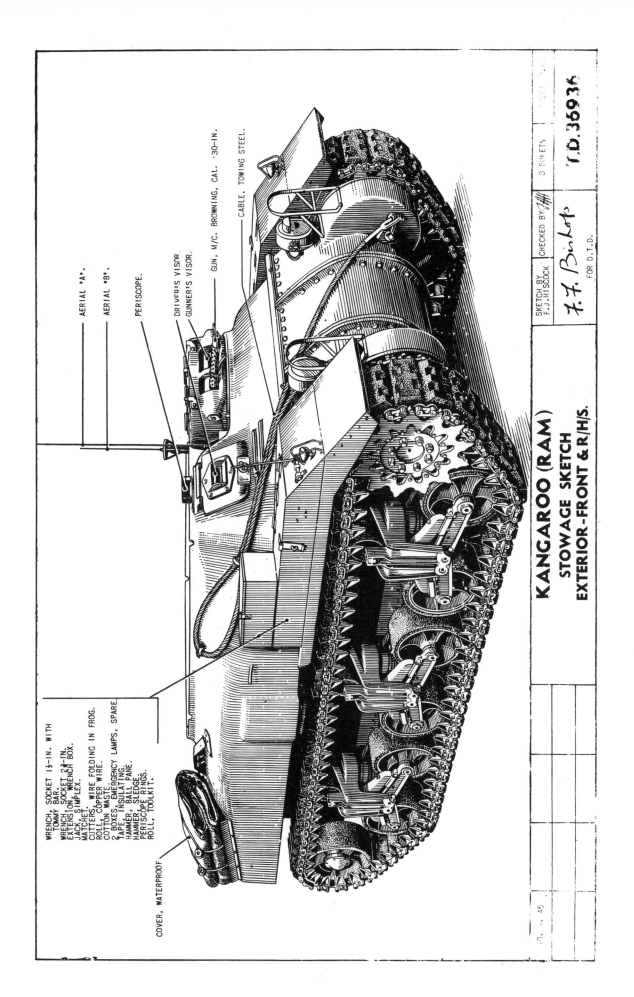

KANGAROO (RAM)

STOWAGE SKETCH
EXTERIOR–FRONT & R/H/S.

AERIAL "A".
AERIAL "B".
PERISCOPE.
DRIVER'S VISOR.
GUNNER'S VISOR.
GUN, M/C. BROWNING, CAL. ·30-IN.
CABLE, TOWING STEEL.

WRENCH, SOCKET 1½-IN. WITH
TOMMY BAR.
WRENCH, SOCKET 2¾-IN.
EXTENSION, WRENCH BOX.
JACK, SIMPLEX.
MATCHET.
CUTTERS, WIRE FOLDING IN FROG.
ROLL, COPPER WIRE.
COTTON WASTE.
2 BOXES, EMERGENCY LAMPS, SPARE.
TAPE, INSULATING.
HAMMER, BALL PANE.
HAMMER, SLEDGE.
PERISCOPE RINGS.
ROLL, TOOLKIT.

COVER, WATERPROOF

SKETCH BY.
F.J.HISCOCK
CHECKED BY.
F.F. Bishop
FOR D.T.D.

3 SHEETS

T.D. 36936

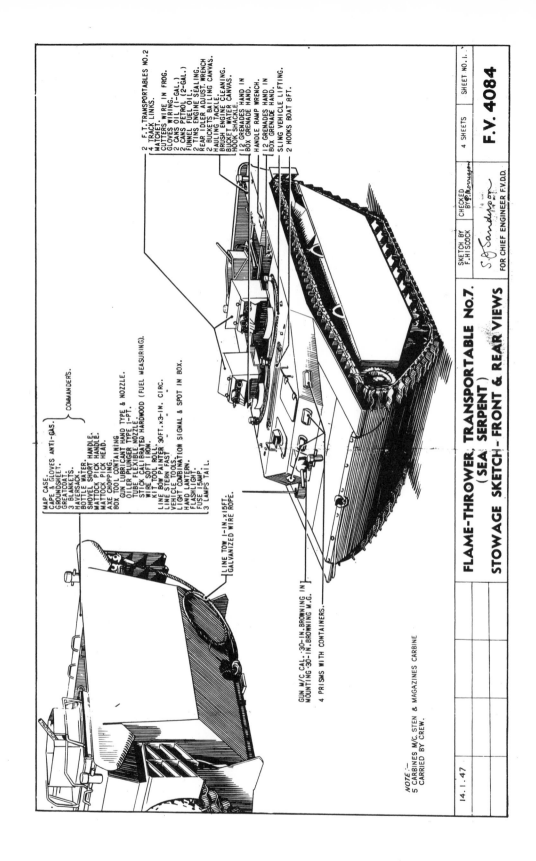

COMMANDERS.
MAP CASE.
CAPE & GLOVES ANTI-GAS.
GROUNDSHEET.
GREATCOAT.
3 BLANKETS.
HAVERSACK.
BOTTLE WATER.
SHOVEL SHORT HANDLE.
MATTOCK PICK HANDLE.
MATTOCK PICK HEAD.
AXE CHOPPING.
BOX TOOL CONTAINING
GUN LUBRICANT HAND TYPE & NOZZLE.
OILER PLUNGER TYPE 1-PT.
TUBE FLEXIBLE NOZZLE.
STICK CALIBRATED HARDWOOD (FUEL MEASURING).
WIRE SOFT IRON.
KIT TOOL R.E. 30FT. x3-IN. CIRC.
LINE BOW PAINTER
LINE STERN FAST   "   "
VEHICLE TOOLS.
LIGHT COMBINATION SIGNAL & SPOT IN BOX.
HAND LANTERN.
FLASHLIGHT.
FUSE 15AMP.
3 LAMPS TAIL.

LINE TOW 1-IN.x15FT.
GALVANIZED WIRE ROPE.

GUN M/C CAL.·30-IN.BROWNING IN
MOUNTING·30-IN.BROWNING M.G.

4 PRISMS WITH CONTAINERS.

2 F.T.TRANSPORTABLES NO.2
4 TRACK LINKS.
MATCHET.
CUTTERS WIRE IN FROG.
GLOVES WIRING.
2 CANS OIL (1-GAL.)
2 CANS PETROL (2-GAL.)
FUNNEL FUEL OIL.
2 TINS ENGINE SEALING.
REAR IDLER ADJUST.WRENCH
2 BUCKETS BAILING CANVAS.
HAULING TACKLE.
BRUSH ENGINE CLEANING.
BUCKET WATER CANVAS.
HOOK SHACKLE.
12 GRENADES HAND IN
BOX GRENADE HAND.
HANDLE RAMP WRENCH.
12 GRENADES HAND IN
BOX GRENADE HAND.
SLING VEHICLE LIFTING.
2 HOOKS BOAT 8FT.

NOTE:--
5 CARBINES M/C STEN & MAGAZINES CARBINE
CARRIED BY CREW.

14.1.47		FLAME-THROWER, TRANSPORTABLE No.7. (SEA SERPENT) STOWAGE SKETCH - FRONT & REAR VIEWS	SKETCH BY F.HISCOCK	CHECKED BY	4 SHEETS	SHEET NO.1.
			S.J.Sandusson FOR CHIEF ENGINEER F.V.D.D.			**F.V. 4084**

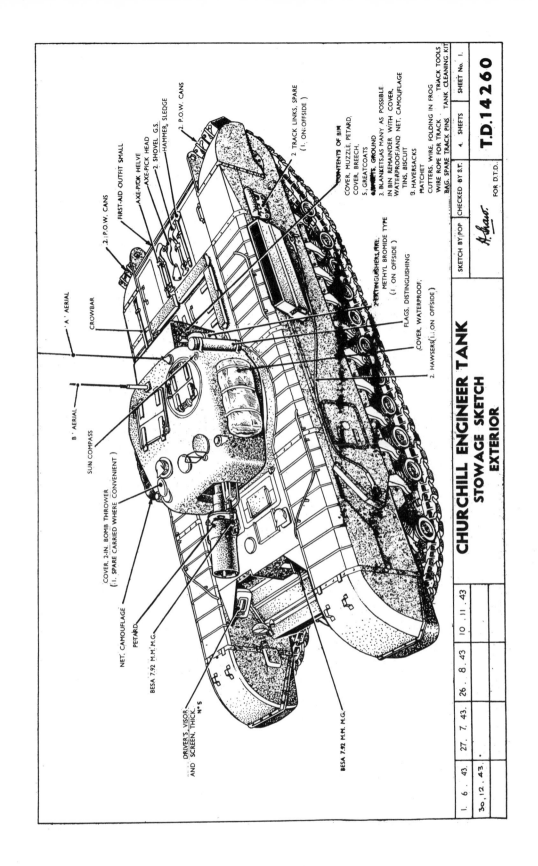

CHURCHILL ENGINEER TANK
STOWAGE SKETCH
EXTERIOR

'A' AERIAL

CROWBAR

2. P.O.W. CANS

FIRST-AID OUTFIT SMALL

AXE-PICK HELVE

AXE-PICK HEAD

2. SHOVEL G.S.

HAMMER, SLEDGE

2. P.O.W. CANS

2. TRACK LINKS, SPARE
(1. ON·OFFSIDE)

CONTENTS OF BIN

COVER, MUZZLE, PETARD,
COVER, BREECH.
5. GREATCOATS
GIMPLETS, GROUND
3. BLANKETS AS MANY AS POSSIBLE
IN BIN REMAINDER WITH COVER,
WATERPROOF, AND NET, CAMOUFLAGE
TINS, BISCUIT
3. HAVERSACKS
MATCHET
CUTTERS, WIRE, FOLDING IN FROG
WIRE ROPE FOR TRACK .
BAG, SPARE TRACK PINS

TRACK TOOLS
TRACK TOOLS
TANK CLEANING KIT

SUN COMPASS

B ' AERIAL

(COVER. 2-IN. BOMB THROWER
(1. SPARE CARRIED WHERE CONVENIENT)

NET, CAMOUFLAGE

PETARD

BESA 7.92 M.M. M.G.

DRIVER'S VISOR
AND SCREEN, THICK. N° 5

BESA 7.92 M.M. M.G.

2. EXTINGUISHERS, FIRE.
METHYL BROMIDE TYPE
(1. ON OFFSIDE)

FLAGS, DISTINGUISHING

COVER, WATERPROOF,

COVER (1. ON OFFSIDE)

2. HAWSERS (1. ON OFFSIDE)

SKETCH BY. POP	CHECKED BY S.T.	4. SHEETS	SHEET No. 1.
	H. Shaw.		**T.D. 14260**
	FOR D.T.D.		

1 . 6 . 43 .	27 . 7 . 43 .	26 . 8 . 43	10 . 11 . 43		
30 . 12 . 43 .					

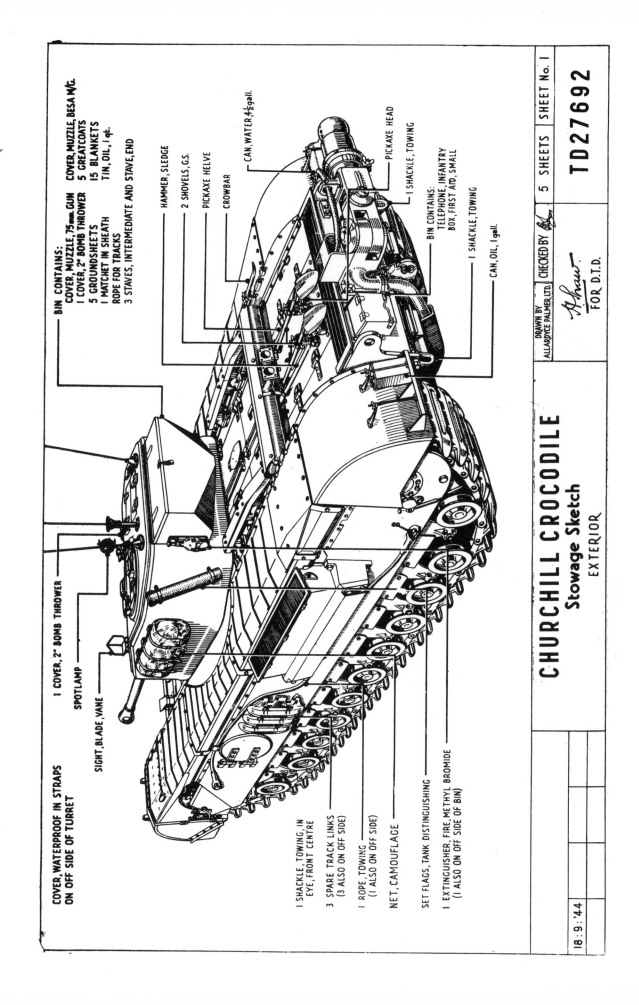

BIN CONTAINS:
COVER, MUZZLE, 75 mm. GUN
1 COVER, 2" BOMB THROWER
5 GROUNDSHEETS
1 MATCHET IN SHEATH
ROPE FOR TRACKS
3 STAVES, INTERMEDIATE AND STAVE, END

COVER, MUZZLE, BESA M/G.
5 GREATCOATS
15 BLANKETS
TIN, OIL, 1 qt.

HAMMER, SLEDGE

2 SHOVELS, G.S.

PICKAXE HELVE

CROWBAR

CAN, WATER, 4½ gall.

PICKAXE HEAD

1 SHACKLE, TOWING

BIN CONTAINS:
TELEPHONE, INFANTRY
BOX, FIRST AID, SMALL

1 SHACKLE, TOWING

CAN, OIL, 1 gall.

COVER, WATERPROOF IN STRAPS
ON OFF SIDE OF TURRET

1 COVER, 2" BOMB THROWER

SPOTLAMP

SIGHT, BLADE, VANE

1 SHACKLE, TOWING, IN
EYE, FRONT CENTRE

3 SPARE TRACK LINKS
(3 ALSO ON OFF SIDE)

1 ROPE, TOWING
(1 ALSO ON OFF SIDE)

NET, CAMOUFLAGE

SET FLAGS, TANK DISTINGUISHING

1 EXTINGUISHER, FIRE, METHYL BROMIDE
(1 ALSO ON OFF SIDE OF BIN)

CHURCHILL CROCODILE
Stowage Sketch
EXTERIOR

DRAWN BY	CHECKED BY	5 SHEETS	SHEET No. 1
ALLARDYCE PALMER LTD.	*A.Shaw* FOR D.I.D.		**TD27692**

18:9:'44

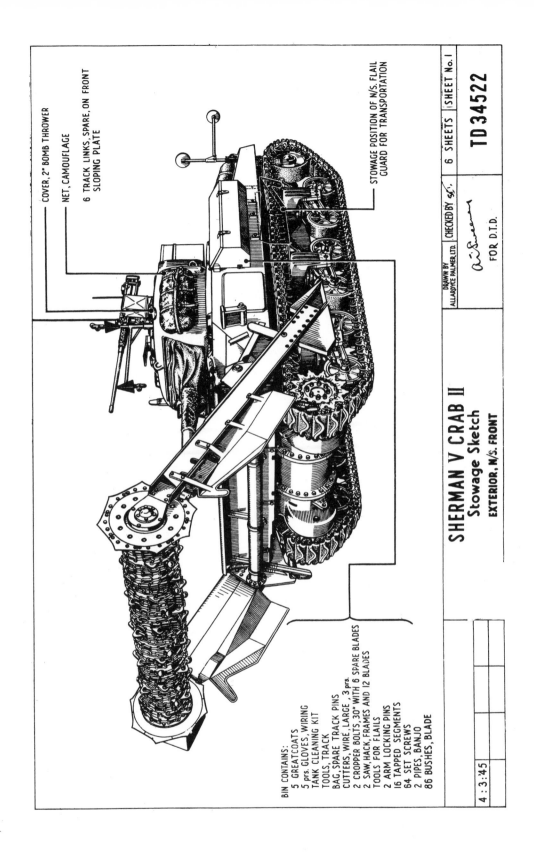

COVER, 2" BOMB THROWER

NET, CAMOUFLAGE

6 TRACK LINKS, SPARE, ON FRONT SLOPING PLATE

STOWAGE POSITION OF N/S. FLAIL GUARD FOR TRANSPORTATION

BIN CONTAINS:
5 GREATCOATS
5 prs. GLOVES, WIRING
TANK CLEANING KIT
TOOLS, TRACK
BAG, SPARE TRACK PINS
CUTTERS, WIRE, LARGE, 3 prs.
2 CROPPER BOLTS, 30" WITH 6 SPARE BLADES
2 SAW, HACK, FRAMES AND 12 BLADES
TOOLS FOR FLAILS
2 ARM LOCKING PINS
16 TAPPED SEGMENTS
64 SET SCREWS
2 PIPES, BANJO
86 BUSHES, BLADE

SHERMAN V CRAB II
Stowage Sketch
EXTERIOR, N/S. FRONT

DRAWN BY ALLARDYCE PALMER LTD.	CHECKED BY 𝓈𝓈.	SHEET No. I
	FOR D.I.D.	6 SHEETS

TD 34522

4 : 3 : 45

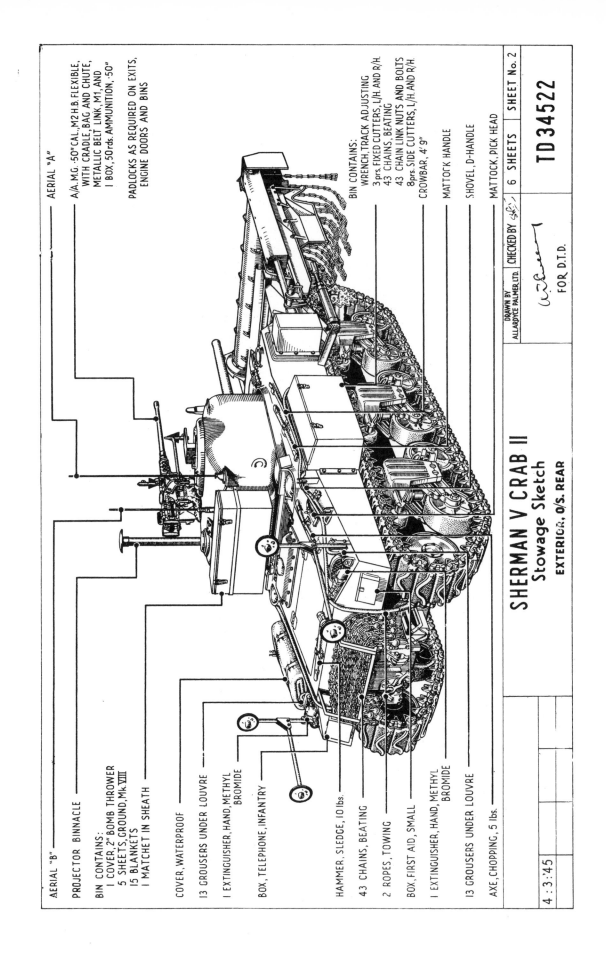

AERIAL "B"

PROJECTOR BINNACLE

BIN CONTAINS:
1 COVER, 2" BOMB THROWER
5 SHEETS, GROUND, Mk.VIII
15 BLANKETS
1 MATCHET IN SHEATH

COVER, WATERPROOF

13 GROUSERS UNDER LOUVRE

1 EXTINGUISHER, HAND, METHYL
BROMIDE

BOX, TELEPHONE, INFANTRY

HAMMER, SLEDGE, 10 lbs.

43 CHAINS, BEATING

2 ROPES, TOWING

BOX, FIRST AID, SMALL

1 EXTINGUISHER, HAND, METHYL
BROMIDE

13 GROUSERS UNDER LOUVRE

AXE, CHOPPING, 5 lbs.

AERIAL "A"

A/A.M.G. .50"CAL.,M2 H.B. FLEXIBLE,
WITH CRADLE, BAG AND CHUTE,
METALLIC BELT LINK, M1, AND
1 BOX, 50 rds. AMMUNITION, .50"

PADLOCKS AS REQUIRED ON EXITS,
ENGINE DOORS AND BINS

BIN CONTAINS:
WRENCH, TRACK ADJUSTING
3 prs. FIXED CUTTERS, L/H. AND R/H.
43 CHAINS, BEATING
43 CHAIN LINK NUTS AND BOLTS
8 prs. SIDE CUTTERS, L/H. AND R/H
CROWBAR, 4'9"

MATTOCK HANDLE

SHOVEL, D-HANDLE

MATTOCK, PICK HEAD

SHERMAN V CRAB II
Stowage Sketch
EXTERIOR, O/S. REAR

4 : 3 :'45	DRAWN BY ALLARDYCE PALMER LTD.	CHECKED BY	6 SHEETS	SHEET No. 2
	FOR D.I.D.		TD 34522	

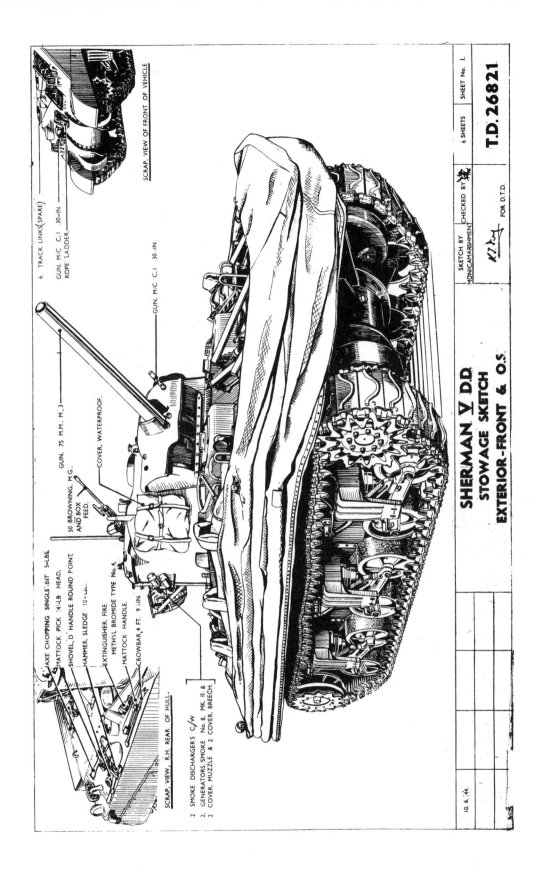

SCRAP. VIEW OF FRONT OF VEHICLE.

6. TRACK LINKS (SPARE)

GUN, M/C C.1 30-IN
ROPE LADDER.

GUN, M/C C.1 30-IN

GUN, 75 M.M. M.3

50 BROWNING, M.G.
AND BOX FEED.

COVER, WATERPROOF.

AXE CHOPPING SINGLE BIT 5-LBS.
MATTOCK PICK 14-LB HEAD.
SHOVEL, D' HANDLE ROUND POINT.
HAMMER, SLEDGE 10-LB.
EXTINGUISHER. FIRE
METHYL BROMIDE TYPE No.4,
MATTOCK HANDLE.
CROWBAR, 4 FT. 9 IN.

SCRAP. VIEW, R.H. REAR OF HULL.

2 SMOKE DISCHARGERS C/W
2. GENERATORS, SMOKE No. 8. MK. II &
2 COVER, MUZZLE & 2 COVER, BREECH.

SHERMAN V D.D.
STOWAGE SKETCH
EXTERIOR-FRONT & O.S.

SKETCH BY MONICAMARSHMENT	CHECKED BY	6 SHEETS	SHEET No. 1.
			T.D. 26821

FOR D.T.D.

10. 6. '44.

83

Glossary

AFV	Armoured Fighting Vehicle
ARK	Turretless tank with ramps, diminutive of ARK ROYAL
ARV	Armoured Recovery Vehicle
AVRE	Armoured Vehicle Royal Engineers
BARON	Minesweeping flail tank
BARV	Beach Armoured Recovery Vehicle
BELCH	Spray device for DD tanks
BOBBIN	Carpet roll attachment for tanks
BUFFALO	British nickname for American LVT
BULLSHORN	Minesweeping plough attachment
CARROT	Mechanical demolition charge placer
CDL	Canal Defence Light
CIRD	Canadian Indestructible Roller Device
CO	Commanding Officer
CONGER	Rocket launched minesweeping device
COXE	Combined Operations Experimental Establishment
CRAB	Sherman tank with minesweeping flail
CROCODILE	Flamethrowing apparatus on Churchill tank
CZECH HEDGHOG	German beach obstacle
DD	Duplex Drive amphibious tank
DUKW	American amphibious truck
ELEMENT C	German beach obstacle
FASCINE	Bundle of sticks for filling ditches etc
FLYING DUSTBIN	High explosive demolition charge for Petard
FUNNIES	British generic term for specialized armour
GIN-AND-IT	Mat laying attachment for DD tanks
GOAT	Mechanical demolition placer
GOC	General Officer Commanding
GREAT EASTERN	Rocket launched ramp on Churchill tank
GROUSERS	Extra wide track shoes fitted for crossing muddy ground
KANGAROO	Turretless tank for transporting infantry
LCT	Landing Craft Tank
LOBSTER	Tank mounted flail device
LSI	Landing Ship Infantry
LVT	Landing Vehicle Tracked
MARQUIS	Tank mounted flail device
MONITOR	Shallow draught, heavy gun naval vessel
OAC	Obstacle Assault Centre
ONION	Mechanical charge placer
PETARD	Large calibre, tank mounted demolition gun
PORPOISE	Amphibious sledge
RAC	Royal Armoured Corps

RAMC	Royal Army Medical Corps
RASC	Royal Army Service Corps
RE	Royal Engineers
REME	Royal Electrical and Mechanical Engineers
RHINO	Self propelled pontoon ferry
RODENT	Lightweight minesweeping device on Weasel
RTR	Royal Tank Regiment
SADE	Specialized Armour Development Establishment
SAE	Specialized Armour Establishment
SBG	Small Box Girder, tank-mounted bridge
SCORPION	Minesweeping flail device
SEA SERPENT	Flamethrowing equipment on LVT
SNAKE	Tubular explosive device for clearing mines
SPUD	Detachable track extensions to improve grip
TAPEWORM	Development of Conger
TERRAPIN	British amphibious truck
TETRAHEDRA	German beach obstacle
TOPEE	Protective screen for DD equipment
WEASEL	Small tracked amphibian
WOODLARK	Rocket launched ARK

Index